Writing Travel Books and Articles

Writing Travel Books and Articles

Richard Cropp
Barbara Braidwood
Susan M. Boyce

Self-Counsel Press
(a division of)
International Self-Counsel Press Ltd.

Printed in Canada

First edition: July 1997

Canadian Cataloguing in Publication Data

Cropp, Richard, 1952-
    Writing travel books and articles

    (Self-counsel series)
    ISBN 1-55180-104-3

    1. Travel writing.   I. Braidwood, Barbara, 1952-   II. Boyce,
Susan M., 1956-   III. Title.   IV. Series.
G151.C76 1997   808'.06691   C97-910229-4

Self-Counsel Press
(a division of)
International Self-Counsel Press Ltd.

Head and Editorial Office	*U.S. Address*
1481 Charlotte Road	1704 N. State Street
North Vancouver, BC V7J 1H1	Bellingham, WA 98225

We dedicate this book with much love to the memory of Sanae Cropp,
who was such an inspiration to us.

R.C. and B.B.

I would like to personally thank the many students
who continue to make teaching creative writing such a joy.
And to Ed, who gently suggested I might enjoy teaching
and then never let me quit, and who continues to be an inspiration
to so many writers and writing teachers.

S.M.B.

Contents

Figures

Checklists

Worksheets

Samples

Acknowledgments

We would like to thank the people who took time to share their experiences and who allowed us to use excerpts of their work and assignments. Special acknowledgment goes to Dick Bellamy (director of photography for *The Beachcombers*, *The Nature of Things*, and many other Canadian Broadcasting Corporation programs and documentaries) for so generously sharing his knowledge of photography.

Introduction

Dawn unfurls her golden glory over the ancient ramparts of Moorea. Your job: watch the sun rise above Cook's Bay from the balcony of your hotel room and capture the delicate first light on film. As you sip fresh pineapple juice and nibble sweet, buttery croissants, you can't help but marvel how the ravages of a volcano could ultimately produce the spectacular beauty of this French Polynesian island.

This afternoon, you'll snorkel in the turquoise lagoon with native Tahitians. You'll hand-feed tiny bait fish to black tip reef sharks and graceful manta rays completely safe, so the guides swear, in nothing but your swimsuit and SPF 40 sunscreen. Later you'll savor a traditional meal of succulent, honey-glazed pig roasted whole on a spit over an open bed of charcoal, followed by pecan pie and rich, dark coffee.

And best of all? The national magazine you're writing an article for is paying you to enjoy this exotic adventure!

All three of us travel the world on someone else's tab and generally live the life of the rich and famous when we aren't home doing dishes and laundry. As travel writers, we have a pocket full of dreams and every chance of fulfilling them.

Imagine landing on a 10,000-year-old glacier for an afternoon picnic lunch, then skiing the slopes of North America's premier ski resort. Even the strudel is an event in this winter paradise!

There's the quiet awe of kayaking under the shadow of burial totem poles in an abandoned Haida Indian village on Canada's rugged northwest coast — a sight guides say few ever experience. Or the incongruity of shivering out on deck in your formal evening wear aboard a luxury cruise liner, as you listen to the thunder of a glacier calving into the ocean off your starboard side.

Nothing can prepare you for the terrifying thrill of flying a laser-equipped military fighter in a dogfight at 10,000 feet. (Thank heavens you didn't have to pay the $2,600 an hour!) Perhaps flying a hot air balloon to chase kangaroos across the Australian outback is more your style.

We've seen and done all these things and more. We've gone skeet shooting in Virginia, bowed our heads in silent respect as we stood in front of the cross marking the spot where the last escapee from

East Berlin was shot down in cold blood before the fall of the Berlin Wall, and discovered firsthand exactly how much can be crammed into a small suitcase after a gala shopping and theater weekend in London, England. All in the name of writing the perfect travel article!

None of us has a journalistic background, and we aren't employed as reporters for big national magazines. We started out just wanting to travel more. We thought becoming travel writers and going to exotic destinations was an unattainable dream, but we've actually been to all these places we mentioned. You can too.

If you read this book and follow our suggestions, we'll show you how you too can have an adventure as unique, romantic, and exciting as any we've experienced. We'll help you get your writing published and give you the inside track on how to get those all-important freebies. Whether you want to write an article or two each year or make a full-time career as a travel writer, this book will give you the benefit of our experience. After that, it's up to you.

Many of the examples given in the book have been drawn from the numerous travel writing classes Susan has taught over the years.

***

Please note: We've been as accurate as possible, but like everything in the travel business, things change. By the time this book goes to press, some information that has remained constant for 20 years will have changed. Rather than relying on this book for every detail, use it as a map to guide you along the road to your own travel writing career. Keep learning, keep writing, and never lose touch with your own sense of wonder about the world around you.

1

Starting out

We are convinced we would be unhappy if we had well-paying jobs outside of travel writing. Of course, we probably wouldn't last long in any case, as we would always be asking for time off to go traveling. And we'd be poor: we'd spend all our income on travel.

Over the last several years we have been offered in excess of $70,000 in free travel each year. To pay for it out of a salary, we would have to earn well over $110,000, before taxes, just to feed our addiction.

If writing and traveling are two of your passions, travel writing will compensate you very well. If you must have most of it in cash, find another profession. The money in travel writing is lousy for most people, mediocre for a few, and spectacular for a tiny minority.

The wonderful thing about travel writing is that you can do as much or as little as you want. Like anything else, the rewards bear some relationship to the effort you expend. For those who look on travel writing as a part-time hobby, keep in mind that few hobbies pay off with a free vacation.

As a career, travel writing is one of the few jobs where the glamorous advance billing actually falls short of the reality. Several times a year, we find ourselves seeing or doing something that our wildest imaginations would not have conjured up before we started as travel writers. While this may say something about our imaginations, travel writing has certainly made our lives a whole lot more interesting.

Not that there isn't a lot of discouraging hard work. This career is no different than any other in that respect. If you are going to be good at travel writing, you will pay your dues. But at some point, with persistence and a little luck, you will find yourself in the most romantic, adventurous, or exciting situations you ever imagined.

But before you can enjoy any of this, you have to get in.

a. Word slave willing to work for free, have computer, will travel...

Unlike many other professions, there isn't a travel writing degree you can earn that automatically qualifies you for a paying job. Most travel writers just start writing travel on a freelance basis, usually part-time and invariably for free, while they learn the ropes.

The competition to be published is so stiff that in the last 20 years just about all the full-time paid travel writer positions have disappeared. Now thousands of amateurs are willing to spend the hours to put together a good story just to see their name in lights.

Syndication has had the same effect. Newspapers can buy a complete article from a syndication service for as little as $5. So an editor is forced to ask what is so special about a freelancer's $200 article, when that editor could fill the same space for next to nothing.

Twenty years ago you could still find a newspaper that would pay freelance journalists for their work and for their tickets to destinations, just to write a story for the paper. Now, what few all-expenses-paid trips still exist are passed secretively from one generation of in-house editors and staff writers to the next. Very few freelancers are hired to write specific stories.

The spectacular increase in the number of good freelance writers willing to write for fame, glory, and a dime a word means you will put in long hours just to have a byline or the chance to learn a new skill or develop a new contact. As a freelancer starting out, what pay you earn will probably just cover expenses — if you receive any money at all.

However, the work has its own reward in the excitement and challenge of stretching yourself, and at least you don't have to pay tuition for this degree in life experience. If you have the time and the initiative, you can pursue the education you need. And, of course, as compensation along the way, you will be invited on a few scrumptious trips.

We have some suggestions for making the most of your time as a word slave.

b. Think small

Set small, realistic goals for yourself. Submit articles to your local paper instead of aiming your queries and articles at *Condé Nast Traveler* or *Islands*. These magazines receive thousands of submissions each year.

Inquire about submitting articles to small travel newsletters. Build yourself a reputation for good work that arrives on time and in the required format. Don't think you can send in 4,000 words when the editors requested 800 to 1,000 and expect them to edit it down. It won't be published.

Worry less about getting paid and more about building a reputation and a list of published works. If you start with small steps, you will eventually get there.

c. Think business

Think of yourself as a business person whose business is writing. The market for people whose only skill is writing is very competitive and low paying. To stand out from your competitors, you must understand the business dimension of what you are doing.

Here's a perfect example from another industry. Who would guess from listening to Loreena McKennitt's harp that she was anything but an ethereal musician. Success obviously came because the music was so inspiring and haunting.

Hardly. Just a few years ago she was playing for change in a subway station. Although McKennitt's music is a pleasure, there are at least a thousand equally talented musicians around the world whose music you will never hear. The difference is McKennitt learned a collection of diverse skills to take advantage of opportunities as they arose. She began by retailing her music at concerts and by mail, using money borrowed from friends and family to finance the project. She taught herself how to negotiate her own contracts, sell overseas rights to her music, and set up and implement complex tours.

McKennitt now runs a bustling office. She keeps her sights set firmly on the future, is aware of what's happening in the music industries of other countries, and has plans for utilizing the Internet. On top of all that, she writes and records some truly beautiful music. McKennitt is successful because she likes the business aspects of her career and spends 80% to 85% of her time on business matters.

Writing good prose may be your most important skill, but to be a success in this industry, it may end up being one of your least used. Writers who view themselves only as writers and refuse to learn about the business are making a huge mistake. With a simple attitude adjustment, you dramatically increase your chances of having your work published.

Further, we guarantee there will be times when you will not be able to earn anything from your writing. Economic recessions, cinched editorial budgets, and travel trends will conspire to keep you out of print at some point. If you have a diversified skill base, you can still be employed doing something in the publishing or writing field, where you are more likely to hear about or develop other projects.

d. Educate yourself

Look for opportunities to learn other skills. Don't restrict yourself to the courses aimed at aspiring writers which are put on by many colleges and universities. Try publishing courses or art and photography courses. Even courses in geography and anthropology will help you write and travel better.

And don't overlook a little business education. Most writers wouldn't be caught dead in a tax course, but the knowledge you gain will save you cash which you can use for other opportunities. Besides, your understanding of taxes might translate into an article at some point.

e. Volunteer

Volunteer anywhere you can where publishing is going on, especially if you are a novice. Real-life educational opportunities are prizes worth spending time and effort to acquire. What they teach about the business of writing and publishing is invaluable and not available through traditional classroom methods.

There are hundreds of publishers of small newsletters, newspapers, and magazines that barely make enough to cover their own salaries. They are always looking for a hand around issue time. Nothing sharpens your ability to find viable commercial projects like working on several different ones and seeing what works and what doesn't. One easy way to do this is to volunteer.

f. Read voraciously

Read, read, read. There are some very helpful magazines and books on writing and on travel. If you can't afford them, ask your local library to subscribe. See the Appendix for a list of publications worth looking at.

Writer's Market: Where and how to sell what you write is a valuable source of information published annually by Writer's Digest Books. Check your library or local bookstores. *Writer's Market* has an extensive list of contact information on book and magazine publishers. As the directory is updated annually, you can depend on it to have relatively current information. However, things change rapidly, so don't expect it to be the final word. We've had letters returned from addresses listed in a current directory.

g. Make your livelihood relevant

You still need to earn a living while you develop your career as a writer. Try to earn your living working in a writing-related industry. As mundane as it may seem, even a stint in a printing plant will teach you lessons about some of the not-so-glamorous aspects of publishing. Years from now, when you have a terrific book idea, you will have part of the foundation for evaluating whether or not you want to self-publish the manuscript. (See also section **c.** above, for a discussion on diversifying your skills.)

h. Think creatively

Using your creativity about your career path can help immensely in this business. Don't be limited by what you think is a traditional path. There is no such thing. Think outrageous thoughts.

Witness the project to research the world's most lethal hot spots, from wars and guerrilla insurgencies to outbreaks of frightening diseases. It was published as a travel guide.

Travel videos, Internet publishing, corporate or tourist board brochure writing, to name a just a few, all require you to be imaginative, will give you practice in your craft, and will open you to other possibilities.

i. Getting rid of that empty mailbox syndrome

Any time you send a request by mail, use it as an opportunity to get your business card out of your wallet and in front of people who could help you build your writing career.

You are going to write on travel, so you need to know what is going on in the world of travel. And how, you might ask, do you get a steady stream of information on the subject arriving at your door or over your fax machine?

You ask for it. Simply call up the company you want information from, speak to someone in the public relations or media relations department, and ask to be put on their media list. Generally it is a very easy task, though you may be shuffled around a bit, but people are usually quite happy to put you on their list. They may ask you to mail or fax a letter with the request. Sample #1 is an example of what to write when requesting information by mail or by fax.

j. Internet publishing

Many publishers don't yet recognize Internet publishing as a valid credential since it's almost impossible to check up on. Words sent out into cyberspace by publishing them on the Net can be, and often are, plagiarized.

To publish or not to publish? When it comes to the Internet, there is still no complete answer: ultimately it will be your personal decision alone that will determine if you want to launch your words into cyberspace.

It is relatively easy to post articles to bulletin boards. Publishing your articles on the Internet gives you an instant audience. Your words will be seen by millions of people worldwide. There is a possibility someone will read your work, decide you absolutely must write for his or her publication or publishing house, and come knocking on your door with a contract in hand. (This actually happened to Diana Gabaldon, a well-known historical romance writer.)

Lee Foster, winner of the Lowell Thomas Travel Journalist of the Year Silver Award, and Carl Purcell, are two well-known travel writers who have successfully begun to exploit this new venue. Working for two of North America's largest information providers, CompuServe and America Online, they have provided articles, travel updates, photographs, and other items of interest to travelers.

Foster points out that "every tourist board with a Web page has someone who manages it." If you can find a sponsor who will pay for your writing time and site management, you may have discovered a new source of income from your travel tales.

123 Your Street
Yourtown, ON J0J 2K8
May 1, 199-

Kristin Caldwell
Media Company ABC
456 Main Street
Anytown MA 86868

Dear Kristin:

I am a freelance travel writer.
Would you please add me to your media list so that I may receive your press
releases and information packages?
My contact information is above.
Thank you.

Sincerely,

Joseph Chan

Joseph Chan

It's almost impossible to find paying markets for an article published on the Internet because there is still no effective method for determining payment. Although there are a handful of magazines produced exclusively on-line (*Omni*, for example), to date we do not know of any travel publications that fall into this category.

If you are technically inclined, you can set up your own magazine or newspaper for a pittance. The attractions are very seductive. There are no printing charges, and distribution is easy and free.

Purcell and Foster both agree that anyone who wants to pursue this market must keep up with last-minute changes in the way electronic media works. The Internet is a fast moving, ever-fluctuating marketplace. But it is a marketplace in its infancy. If you are looking for excitement and a challenge that won't get stale, Internet publishing may be exactly what you're after.

Unfortunately, the same commercial rules that apply to their printed cousins apply to electronic magazines. At some point you want to make money to cover all the time it takes to write and lay out such a publication, as well as to pay your writers.

Subscribers are actually harder to obtain because they are so used to free information on the Internet. Many sites that have survived for a few years have done so with the help of advertising. They have managed to convince tight-fisted, cagey advertising executives that people don't just hit on the publication's site and move on but actually take the time to read messages from the sponsors.

Publishing articles or creating an entire publication will give you some valuable feedback and experience. But there is a disadvantage. Many people are very wrapped up in the Internet. All that interaction is seductive. Despite the hype and promise, 99.5% of people still obtain most of their information on travel from mainstream sources. Or they read it the old-fashioned way.

k. Starting a newsletter or a magazine

We love newsletters as a first publishing effort. Magazines we don't. The difference between the two is the amount of financial risk you must take to achieve exactly the same thing. Both endeavors will teach you the business of writing and publishing, but a newsletter of, say, 12 pages, put out four to six times a year, can be 20 to 30 times cheaper than putting out a magazine that same number of times.

Magazines are more expensive for a number of reasons. They have more pages than a newsletter, which means added cost for writing, editing, and printing. Distribution can cost more, especially by mail: the more the publication weighs, the more it costs to ship. However, by far the biggest difference between a magazine and a newsletter is in the production costs. With a newsletter, anyone with a word processor is in business. If there are any pictures at all, readers expect that they will be black and white, and somewhat grainy. Travel magazines, on the other hand, must be in full color to attract advertisers. The color production and printing process is several times the cost per page of a black-and-white newsletter.

You don't learn 20 to 30 times as much for the extra financial risk, except maybe how to deal with massive stress. You still need to gather ideas, research and write articles, do a little layout, and figure out how to create a saleable product and deliver it. These things will be helpful for future projects, regardless of how the newsletter venture turns out. Best of all, it's really hard to hurt yourself financially with a newsletter.

If you have success, expand it slowly. Newsletters can become respected vehicles for delivering timely travel writing to the public. Consumers Union publishes *Consumer Reports Travel Letter*, which has a wide following; *Thrifty Traveler* reports on general travel tips in a well-researched, chatty way.

Try to find a niche. *TravelTips* has been around for years reporting on freighter travel. *Travel Impulse* is well known for reporting on courier flights. There are newsletters about the food in France, sailing the Caribbean, specific destinations, and any other travel subject you can think of. And there is still room for more.

If you can find a niche for your newsletter that is not filled, or even better, a unique marketing plan combined with an old idea, you are on your way. All you need to do to start is publish the first issue. No hunting for start-up capital, no formal business plan (although you should have a good marketing plan in your head), no employees to hire, no government red tape, and no big equipment purchases.

As a side benefit, you don't need to worry about keeping your writing skills from atrophying while you try to find a publisher for your work: you have a guaranteed outlet for all you can write. (How big your market actually is, is a different problem.)

With guaranteed publication, you will find that despite your newsletter being small, you will still be invited on press trips and to travel seminars. As a publisher, you will have more opportunities than as just a freelancer. To get going, and for pointers on production and marketing, see *Producing a First-Class Newsletter,* another title in the Self-Counsel Series.

l. Buying a byline

We have occasionally heard of writers offering an article to a publication, with the additional offer of paying the publication to print it. And we know of at least once when this has worked. The article was good, the author needed some publication credits quickly and had money to burn. Voila! Instant bio. (Chapter 13 discusses in more detail how to write a bio.)

A wrinkle on this theme: it is fairly common for an advertiser in a magazine to want some editorial when it pays for an ad. Travel writers have been known to pay for ads on the condition that one of their stories runs in the same issue.

We know this is offensive to some writers who think journalistic integrity is paramount, but it is a fact of the real writing world. Don't dismiss the idea out of hand.

Magazines of all stripes, from one-million-subscriber monthlies to tiny newsletters, survive on the ad-for-editorial exchange. Despite cries of outrage to the contrary, all you need to do is look at many magazines' advertising and then look at who gets a mention in the editorial. (Check the issue before and after that ad, too.)

In one sense, paying for an article to appear isn't any worse than buying or starting a newspaper or magazine and then writing the editorial. Most writers don't think this a crime. The only caveat about this short cut is that you can't talk about it: some frown on this deeply. It is hypocritical, but that's the way it is.

Also, many writers trying to build a bio volunteer to help a magazine get started, with the implicit understanding that one or more of their articles will be published. The magazine gets free grunt work and the writers get bylines. We're not sure we see the distinction between paying with money or paying with noble writing sweat.

2
Categories, classifications, and other capers

a. Categories of travel writing

One the most exciting aspects of travel writing is that there are as many different ways of describing the world as there are travel writers. Give ten people an assignment to write about the Yucatán peninsula in Mexico and you will end up with ten entirely different stories — guaranteed. This is known as a writer's voice and is something you will develop automatically the more you write.

However, there are some specific categories of travel writing; knowing what they are can help both as you write and as you market your work. Here is a general list of the most basic types of travel writing. Be aware that almost all of these can and should overlap to some degree. The categories are meant as broad outlines only, not as immovable boundaries where elements of one can never cross paths with another.

1. Destination pieces

Probably the most popular and common type of travel writing, destination pieces are the foundation of most travel writing, whether they are article or book length. Just as the name implies, destination pieces describe a specific place or attraction. They should leave the reader feeling they have just enjoyed a mini-vacation without ever leaving home. Destination pieces are often the cause of out-of-the-blue phone calls to travel agents.

2. First-person travel tales

First-person accounts of foreign travel never seem to lose their popularity. A century later, people still follow in the steps of Robert Louis Stevenson (well-loved author of such great children's classics as *Kidnapped* and *Treasure Island*) as he tramped through France in the late 1800s writing *Travels With a Donkey*.

First-person pieces allow a certain amount of introspection, the author's musings and personal comments adding a unique charm to this type of travel writing. Just be sure you avoid the dreaded "What I did on my summer vacation" story. These first-person accounts are no more popular today than they were on the first day of class back in elementary school.

3. Specialty themes

There are a host of magazines that focus exclusively on one aspect of travel. *Cruise Travel Magazine*, *RV Times Magazine*, and *St. Maarten Nights* are only three. Their names tell exactly what readers can expect to find inside. But almost any general travel magazine or newspaper travel section is also a potential market for theme pieces ranging from the pubs of Cornwall to B&Bs of the Virgin Islands.

4. Reviews

A relative of specialty themes, reviews are frequent flyers among travel writing opportunities: hotels, restaurants, museums and other attractions, bus tours, festivals — the list is endless. Reviews benefit everyone. From the writer's perspective, they often mean free or reduced admission in addition to whatever is earned from the sale of the actual writing. The attraction itself gains advertising. And the reader is let in on up-to-the-minute insider information.

5. Guide books

There are many magazines devoted to history and some (such as Historic Traveler*) even specialize in travel. Check the various writers' listings for more.*

Guide books are basically informational only. While there may be a few anecdotal stories, readers buy guide books because they want hard facts about a destination: how to get there, where to stay, what the climate is like, what language is spoken. Some authors, such as Fodor and Steves, have made entire careers of writing nothing but guide books.

6. Historical travel

Some destinations almost shout the word "History!" The Parthenon, the Egyptian pyramids, Custer's Battlefield — try visualizing any of these without thinking of their history. While everywhere *has* a history, sometimes a destination *is* its history.

7. Travel-related topics

Almost every travel magazine and newspaper travel section needs tidbits of information to fill those small, leftover blank spots on the page. While travel-related topics can often be the source of articles in their own right, don't overlook their potential to generate a steady stream of fillers. Here's a brief sampling of ideas:

(a) Health tips for travelers

(b) Traveling with pets

(c) Safety abroad

(d) Traveling solo

(e) Tips for disabled travel

(f) Packing tips

(g) Courtesy abroad

(h) Foreign customs procedures

(i) Getting directions when you can't speak the language

(j) Travel insurance

The list is limited only by your imagination. Travel-related topics can be an interesting sideline or regular income earner.

b. Market categories

In addition to these general writing categories, there are four market categories you need to be aware of: newspapers, consumer publications, trade publications, and books.

1. Newspapers

Newspapers come in all sizes. Some are only a few pages long; you can browse through them in five to ten minutes. Others amount to a daily tome worthy of at least a full pot of coffee accompanied by a generous plate of your favorite cookies. The one thing these newspapers have in common is a thirst for newsworthy stories. Even small-town papers often run a regular travel feature on the weekends, and most dailies in large, urban centers have a separate travel section.

2. Consumer publications

Consumer publications are what most people think of when they hear the word "magazine." But don't be fooled into thinking you can write only for consumer magazines that specialize in travel. For example, some of the best magazine markets for travel articles are seniors' publications because today's seniors travel more extensively than their counterparts of half a century ago. Other consumer magazines worth checking out include:

(a) Bridal (a romantic honeymoon is part of almost every wedding)

(b) Young professional publications

(c) Women's magazines

(d) Nature/natural history

(e) Historical

(f) Outdoor sports and recreation

(g) Auto club members' magazines

(h) City and regional magazines

Even food magazines can be a potential market. We once pitched an idea for a review of a vegan B&B to a leading vegetarian magazine. They sent us back a polite decline explaining they had sent a staff writer there only a month and a half prior to receiving our query letter. If our timing had been only slightly better, we might have sold the article.

3. Trade publications

Trade publications, also known as technical or professional journals, are often overlooked as a market for travel writing. However, the 1996 edition of *Writer's Market* (published annually by Writer's Digest Books) lists three strong advantages of trade publications: "writers who *have* discovered trade journals have found a market that offers the chance to publish regularly in subject areas they find interesting, editors who are typically more accessible than their commercial counterparts, and pay rates that rival those of the big-name magazines."

When you're approaching the trade market, be sure to tie your idea to the particular profession. An article on Spanish monasteries might work for an architectural magazine if the focus is how they were built, rather than why they were built.

4. Books

Travel books are a tough, but not impossible, sell. Like any major project, a travel book will take longer to write than a series of articles, but if this is where your writing heart is, don't be scared off. Simply recognize that the time it takes to write and market tends to remain proportional — if it takes longer to write, in most cases it will also take longer to market.

c. The four elements of travel articles

1. The words you use to tell your story

> Words have weight, sound, and appearance; it is only
> by considering these that you can write a sentence
> that is good to look at and good to listen to.
>
> W. Somerset Maugham, "The Summing Up"

The single most important part of any travel article is, of course, the choice of words you use. People everywhere love to hear stories, but if the stories are hard to follow, the descriptions bland, and the grammar "creative," you won't keep your audience for long. In this book, we'll give you a lot of tips to improve your writing, plus a number of exercises to help you clarify the focus of your travel articles.

2. Photography and travel articles

Perhaps no other type of writing is so inextricably linked with photography as travel writing is. Most people who read a destination piece feel at least mildly cheated if there are no pictures to accompany the words. Your words must paint a picture, but photographs will dramatically increase your chances of enticing an editor to accept your work.

"But I don't know the first thing about photography. All I've ever done is take snapshots of my family and friends!" you may be saying. Don't panic. There are many, many magazines that happily accept a selection of "snapshot quality" photographs to accompany an article. Some even prefer them, as they tend to be folksier and therefore, somehow more real. And for those of you who want more, chapter 5 will help you with all the basics you need to get started down the road to photos with flair.

3. Sidebars

Imagine becoming engrossed in a warm, cuddly article about panda bear cubs in China. You can feel the soft, black and white fur beneath your fingertips. A tear escapes your eye as you visualize the look of love passing between parent and child. You're ready to hop on the next plane and join the fight to preserve these remarkable, nearly extinct creatures.

Suddenly, an unexpected list of cold, hard statistics intrudes:

(a) Number of reserves in China: 14

(b) Decline in number of wild pandas worldwide during last ten years: approximately 50%

(c) Number of times pandas have been successfully bred in captivity by Chinese people: 28

(d) Fee charged by Chinese zoos to loan a panda for several months: up to $500,000

While this information adds important credibility to your article, the mood is shattered.

The solution? Write a sidebar.

Sidebars are boxes labeled anything from "If You Go" to "FYI" or even "Important Stats." They accompany many travel articles and are a standard way of inserting information that would otherwise break the flow or mood of the piece. Readers can finish reading your article before they have to digest numbers, directions, or other "dry" information, or, if they can't wait, they can read the sidebar right away.

4. Dressing up the package

There are endless possibilities for adding extras to enhance your travel article. Maps, diagrams, ticket stubs, pages from an ancient journal or diary, plaques and certificates of merit . . . the list goes on.

A good rule of thumb: when you're traveling or researching an article, collect as much material as you possibly can. It's a lot easier to pick the best from a dozen menu samples you picked up en route than it is to go back to that great little restaurant in Greece once you've returned home.

Computer technology has also made an ever increasing supply of first-rate photos, illustrations, and travel clip art readily available to anyone with a CD-ROM. While most professional publications will have their own libraries of this window dressing, electronically available material can provide an inexpensive backup you can offer to smaller publications.

One word of caution though. If you are using copies of other people's work, be sure to obtain the appropriate permission before using it. We discuss copyright, release forms, and other legal issues further in chapter 18.

3
A thousand and one ideas

*The most beautiful thing in the world is, of course,
the world itself.*

Wallace Stevens, F. Doggett, and R. Buttel

Ideas are everywhere. From the moment we wake up to the moment
we close our eyes at day's end, they surround us, ready to be gathered,
savored, and turned into stories. And yet, many people still ask,
"Exactly where do you writers come up with all your ideas?"

The classic, if irreverent, cocktail party answer is, "Every year, I
pay $9.95 to a pack of elves in a small town in Colorado, and they
send me ten new ideas each month in a plain envelope." The truth
is, most writers pick up more ideas than they can possibly use simply
by walking down a street — even a street in their hometown.

Try substituting the word "interesting" for the word "beautiful"
in the quote above, and you'll begin to see how travel writers make
a living. Here are some suggestions to save you the $9.95 a month.

a. Traveling doesn't have to be foreign — developing the opportunities in your own backyard

High on many people's list of excuses not to write is, "But I've never
been anywhere exciting. How can I write a travel article?"

We often forget that everywhere on the face of the earth is a
foreign, exciting destination to someone. The good old hometown
where we were born and raised is a place of mystery and adventure

to someone seeing it for the first time. Unfortunately, it's easy to become used to the place we live. Natural beauty, unique architecture, art, culture, or historical significance — all become commonplace when we spend most days preoccupied with downtown traffic jams and grocery shopping.

We are fortunate to live in what is now recognized worldwide as one of the most beautiful cities in North America: Vancouver, British Columbia. People who visit here are awed by the mountains, ocean, and incredible diversity of people. And yet, unless we have out-of-town guests, we often go two or three years without visiting Stanley Park, one of the undisputed "must sees" on any visitor's list.

Even if you've never ventured far beyond your hometown, by re-awakening the same excitement a first-time visitor feels, you'll find a never-ending source of articles suitable for markets across the country (or across the globe).

Here are some ways to get you started exploring the wonders of your own backyard for travel writing ideas.

By honing your skills writing about a destination you're familiar with, you'll also become more aware of the things you need to remember when visiting unknown lands.

(a) Take a day tour. In any major center and a surprising number of small towns, there are local companies that conduct guided tours lasting anywhere from two to eight hours. Guides are selected for their personality as well as their knowledge of the area, so you can be sure you'll have an enjoyable interlude in addition to learning something new about the place you call home.

Give yourself permission to think and act like a tourist during your day out. Pretend you're seeing everything for the first time. Ask a lot of questions, even the "typical tourist" ones. What interests you? What interests everyone else on the tour? This is a great way to find ideas for articles.

(b) Head for a popular tourist spot or a place where people congregate, and eavesdrop as you walk down the street. Listen for foreign accents and languages around you. What brings out an "Oooh!" of excitement and what causes nothing beyond a blank look of disinterest? The "Ooohs" are automatic tip-offs and often something quite unexpected.

For example, when we were organizing a city tour for a group of New York editors and publishers, we expected that the giant Haida carving taking up temporary residency in a local gallery would be a highlight. Not so. It received polite but superficial reviews. The attraction which hands-down won the prize for most-talked-about was a ten-minute ride aboard a small ferry that bobbed back and forth across an inland harbor known as False Creek. Cost for the ride? $1.75 each.

By simply listening to the reactions and conversations around us, we discovered an unexpected story potential.

(c) Convince your favorite relative to come for a visit, even if it's only an imaginary one. Create a plan to show off the town and surrounding area you live in. Actively thinking about what you are proud of will help you focus on what sets *your* "backyard" aside from the town down the road — exactly the skill you need to develop when you see a destination for the first time. And it's almost guaranteed that when you look for them, you'll be amazed just how many exceptional things about home get lost in the haze of day-to-day living.

(d) Talk to travel agents and other travel professionals. What attractions do people always want to include in their visit?

(e) An unusual source of ideas can often be found by chatting with the staff at local shops and garages. Don't forget these public relations specialists are on the front line, day after day, fielding questions from tourists. Their real-life tales are often hilarious: the woman who wanted to know how high above sea level she would be during a 15-minute ocean ferry ride is just one. The questions may seem a bit off the wall, but they can point out subjects that need to be addressed as you market your home-grown travel tales to far away places.

b. Brainstorming

It used to be considered trendy or "new age mumbo jumbo," but today brainstorming has become recognized as one of the best tools for generating ideas. The subject can be as familiar as a favorite sweater and a warm blanket by a fireplace or as exotic as trekking through the Himalayas with only non-English speaking guides for company. Brainstorming inevitably opens unexpected avenues for any type of writing because it encourages fluid, non-linear thinking.

Many prestigious, high-profile corporations of every description use brainstorming for problem solving. So think of yourself joining ranks with members of the Fortune 500 group as you settle down to a rousing session of brainstorming.

Also known as webbing, brainstorming is nothing more than encouraging your mind to play with and expand an idea. It works best with three or more people, but can certainly be done on your own. It's fun, always ends up producing at least one or two good laughs, and inevitably brings so many ideas to light that you'll stop wondering where to find ideas and start worrying about which ones to work on first.

We often use brainstorming when we're looking for new ideas to write about or when we're stumped on exactly what part of a trip to single out for an article.

A number of years ago, Susan was in Ashland, Oregon, attending the Oregon Shakespeare Festival. For any theater buff, it would have been three days of heaven. And yet, when she sat down to write the article, to her horror, she discovered she couldn't get going. She couldn't find her focus. A couple of hours passed by. She was still staring at a blank computer screen, although there was now a small stack of crumpled paper on the floor beside her — failed first drafts and openings which had produced some amazing gibberish but nothing publishable.

Finally, she grabbed a blank sheet of paper, and after no more than five minutes of solid brainstorming, had not only recalled half a dozen small details she'd forgotten, but had realized the trip's true highlight had been the performance of Hamlet. After that, the article all but wrote itself.

Here are some of the keys to effective brainstorming:

(a) Adopt an "anything goes, no censorship" attitude. No matter how unrelated, unusual, or out-and-out weird a thought might seem, there is no such thing as a good or bad response during this exercise. In one brainstorming session, we started with Arizona, progressed through outdoor sports to golf, then to golf widows and some miserable if hilarious divorce stories, and finally to sailing around the world on a private yacht.

   Everything is a potential idea. Don't question *why* keys and a car suddenly make you think of a waterfall. Accept that they do, and allow your mind to pursue the new thought. Who knows where you'll end up.

(b) Never attempt to brainstorm on a computer. No matter how fast you can type, there is a different mental process and connection with handwritten words. A computer also makes it almost impossible to jump back and forth between topics as you think of other things; using a computer will force you into a more linear thought process, which is exactly what this exercise is designed to bypass.

(c) Write as fast as you can; speed helps generate even more ideas.

(d) Put each word or thought in a circle or box instead of listing each one in a rigid line, or below one another. It is much easier to expand an idea when all you need to do is draw a line, a new circle, and write down the new thought. If you run out of space where you're working, just draw a new line to a blank section of the page.

Figure #1 shows how one student brainstormed around the far-too-broad and vague topic of "Hawaii." The Hawaiian islands have been the subject of endless books, and there's still more to write about them. The student's web allowed her to focus on several narrowly defined subjects within the broad topic. Her article ultimately focused on underwater photography, a subject on one of the outer edges of her web and one she might have missed otherwise.

c. One picture can generate 1,000 words

Photos and other illustrations are another readily-at-hand source of inspiration. Go through your photo album and really look at the things you've photographed over the years. Don't worry about composition or whether you have dozens of photos of the aunties and almost none of the cousins. The purpose is to discover what local attractions you thought were worthwhile to show off to your relatives.

1. Theme

Do you see any recurring themes in your photographs? Perhaps most of your pictures show the river or the wide-open plains stretching into the background. Maybe someone is always leaning against the front door of a heritage building or peering through the display cases of museums. Or maybe you feature children's activities and entertainment — playgrounds, amusement parks, or street magicians and clowns.

Themes in your photography can be a tip-off to things you can use as themes in your writing. Especially when you're starting out, write about what interests you. As any parent will tell you, there is a huge

Figure #1
Brainstorming

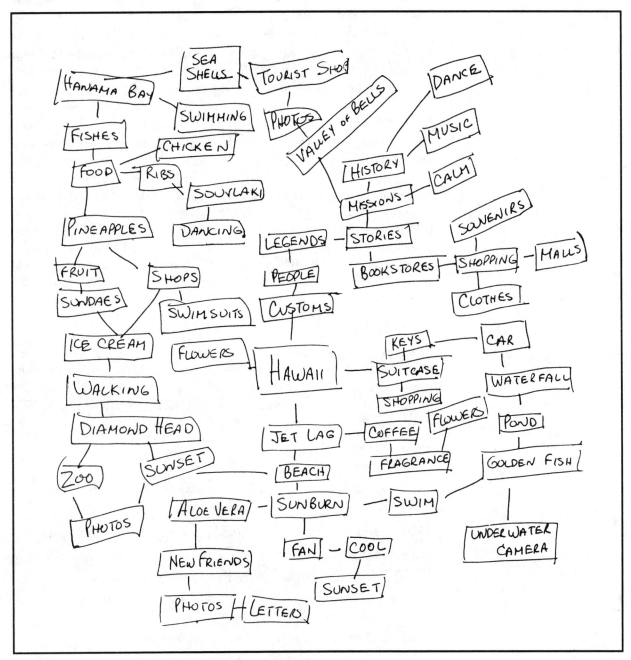

This figure reproduced courtesy of M.M.Brown.

market for ideas on how to keep the kids entertained during the family vacation. So, if you're passionate about children's entertainment, look for ways to incorporate it into your writing and send your query letter (see chapter 9) to the travel section of a good parenting magazine.

However, if babysitting your best friend's two-year-old for a couple of hours stretches the limits of your patience, don't attempt to write an article on the local children's festival.

2. Tone

What about the tone of your photos? A sailboat drifting into the sunset creates a completely different mood than the hustle and bustle of a street market. If you're attracted to pastoral tranquillity, begin by concentrating on those aspects of your hometown. Perhaps there is a botanical garden, a monastery, an artist's retreat, or even a celestial observatory in your town. Any of these could be worthy topics for a travel article. And because they are in keeping with your own personality, you will likely find they make the first steps in your writing career easier than writing about the newly built motorcycle racetrack.

3. Details

When you look at your pictures, what do you want to know more about? One writing class exercise is to use a blow-up of the photograph in Figure #2. Working in groups, the students decide what parts of the image they would like to have more details about. The list normally includes questions such as these:

(a) What kind of ship is it?

(b) Where is it sailing?

(c) What are the people at the railing taking pictures of?

(d) Is there particular significance to the plaid blankets?

(e) Who or where is the person missing from the first seat?

(f) What time of year is it?

(g) Why is the person in the third seat reading a map?

(h) Do these people know each other? Is it a group traveling together, or strangers who just met?

(i) Is there really a glacier in the background?

(j) How many people can fit in each life raft?

Figure #2
Photo used for writing exercise

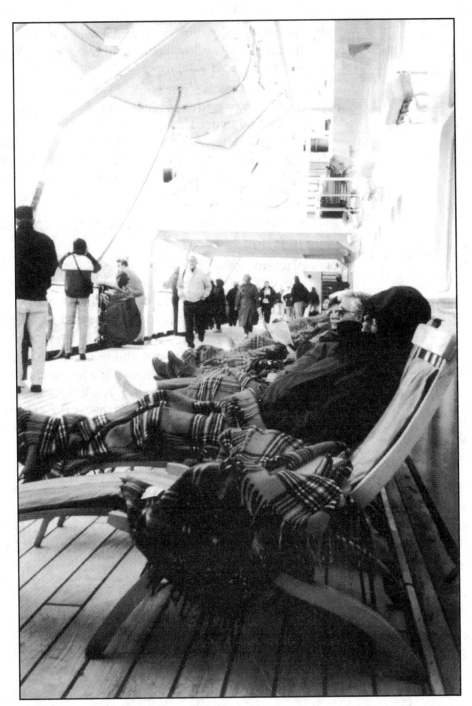

If something raises a question in your mind, it will probably raise questions in your readers' minds too. Your own curiosity is a great place to begin planning travel writing.

While not all these questions will develop easily into travel stories, any can be used as a starting point for a brainstorming web.

4. Clip and keep

A clipping file is an invaluable resource when scrounging for writing ideas. Whether it's reading the daily newspaper or flipping through junk mail, be a voracious clipper.

Anything that catches our fancy, from a short filler on a museum devoted entirely to undergarments (it's true, check out the Lingerie Museum in Hollywood) or the latest Web site for our favorite ski resort, gets tossed in a box under our desks. Once a month or so, we go through and sort these treasures into the filing cabinet. When we think we're short on ideas, we've got hundreds ready and waiting at our fingertips.

5. Always carry a mental butterfly net to capture ideas fluttering by

For a place to hone your ability in really "seeing" with a travel writer's eye, your own backyard makes a perfect classroom. It's easily accessible (after all, you live right there), many things will cost nothing more than the time spent looking, and you can always make a return trip.

Devote time to enhancing your ability to really see the wonders in your surroundings, wherever you are. It's fun, gives you a great step forward in your travel writing, and you'll find yourself constantly amazed by the beauty and diversity of the world around us. And that amazement is exactly the stuff good travel writing is made of.

4

The writing process —
from inspiration to creation

a. Anatomy of an outline

Outline. The mere word strikes terror into the hearts of many new, and a surprising number of not-so-new, travel writers. Some blanche; some develop twitches or abruptly change the subject; many suppress a shudder or flat out say they never use one. "Oh, I don't need one of *those*. I have it all mapped out in my head."

But just as most people wouldn't dream of driving through a strange city without a current map to help them find their final destination, most professional writers don't begin a project without an outline to show them the direction they should be taking next.

Advantages to working with an outline:

(a) You never have to wonder what you're going to write about next, especially on those days when you're feeling less than inspired or longing to be sitting on the beach instead of writing about it.

(b) An outline will give you a good idea of how long a particular writing project will take. If you know you need to write four sections of 1,500 words each to complete your outline, simply multiply the time it takes you to write 1,500 words by four, look at when your deadline is, and you'll be able to decide if you can really afford the time to go to that great sounding movie or all-night party.

An outline is a writer's guide as he or she navigates through writing anything from a 500-word hotel review to a 500-page historical history of Paris.

(c) If you need to make changes to the flow (order) so a piece sounds better or to accommodate some fabulous, newly discovered piece of information, the outline is the easiest place to make those changes. Once they're added into the outline, making changes in the manuscript itself is simple.

(d) As you break a large writing project down into smaller sub-sections, your outline will do double duty as a checklist to make sure you haven't forgotten anything and haven't duplicated subjects.

(e) Outlines help you focus on exactly what your article or book is about. One of the most common errors many writers make is to set up an article discussing a destination's castles, food, castles, beaches, culture, food, castles, culture, music, and then castles again. This kind of subject hopping is guaranteed to encourage even the most devoted reader to put down the magazine or book and move on to a more logical piece.

Creating a basic outline is much simpler than many people realize. There are only three essential elements: the same three elements found in any good piece of writing.

In most travel writing classes, students will hem and haw when asked to suggest what they think those three elements are. Eventually, someone usually says, with a bit of a snigger, "Beginning, middle, and end?" A ripple of laughter goes through the classroom as if something so outrageously simple and obvious couldn't possibly be the definition of the "Mythical and Mysterious Outline."

However, the laughter subsides quickly when everyone realizes these three items are the basics of any outline, no matter what the size or type of the project.

Outlines aren't nearly as scary or difficult as many people believe. They are a malleable, nonjudgmental tool, so forget about the highly structured and almost totally inflexible outlines probably forced on you during high school. The same way your writing will reflect your individuality, an outline will reflect your own personality and working style.

There really is no right or wrong way to create an outline. Most people find point form to be the easiest way of putting together an effective outline. They jot down the basics and then expand and organize them into a working whole. But don't let that intimidate you if you prefer grammatically correct sentences. If you like a very formalized outline style, neatly laid out as a separate computer file, that's okay too. Go for it.

As a rule of thumb, the more complex (which generally equates to the longer) your writing project, the more you need an outline to keep you on track, help you avoid forgetting important items, and prevent you from wandering back and forth through the various points you are making or the details you are describing.

b. Great beginnings — how the west is won or lost

> As we walked along the cobblestone driveway up to the front of our hotel, my traveling companion and I noticed the hot Phoenix heat.

Are you bored yet? If you aren't, you can be sure your readers will be. You've wasted 24 words saying nothing. You've even managed to say nothing twice — of course heat is hot!

> Shimmering like a veiled Arabian heiress in the desert heat, our Phoenix hotel danced seductively among giant palms, luring us down the cobblestone drive.

Both these examples use the same number of words — count them. Twenty-four in each case. But the second example not only creates a mood for this piece (we would expect a fairly lyrical piece focusing on the exotic luxury of the hotel property), it even gives us additional information. In the first version, we don't hear about the palm trees.

Most writers find crafting a strong lead the most difficult part of the writing process. And yet, the opening hook is your first and usually your only chance to make the sale. Whether your audience is an editor who may buy the article or someone who is considering buying some good Saturday morning reading, it's critical to capture your reader's interest immediately with your opening.

One editor we spoke to recently said if an author hasn't hooked her within the first three paragraphs, she puts the manuscript on the rejection pile. Another was slightly more generous and allowed two double-spaced pages. We've also heard, "Grab me in the first three sentences or forget it."

It's easy to fall into the trap of constantly revising your outline to avoid starting your project. Your outline should be a tool to help you reach one end, and one end only: getting the article or book written.

Spend time getting your opening right. It's usually your only chance to grab an editor's attention.

29

Your opening must give a clear and honest idea of what the article is going to be about. A surefire way of turning off your readers and your editors is to open with a subject and then fail to follow through.

A classic example is from a student who turned in an assignment with a catchy opening describing the sounds and smells of a riverside barbecue — the sizzle, the charcoal smoke, the laughter of children dancing through the waves in the river.

Unfortunately, the article turned out to be about three tulip farms. The tulip farms would have made a good article (especially as she had some excellent photos to go with it), but she had set her readers up to expect a piece about salmon barbecues. At the end, we felt cheated because she had failed to give us what she had promised in her opening. Besides, there was nowhere to get barbecued salmon at two o'clock in the morning.

While some of the best openings defy definition — their very uniqueness is what makes them appealing — there are a number of standard leads. Understanding how and why they work will help you develop your own irresistible openings.

1. Use a relevant and interesting saying or quotation

We like to keep several good quotation books handy — the more unusual the better. Some, like The Oxford Dictionary of Quotations, we've bought new at full price. Most of the ones we use frequently, we've picked up at garage sales or hole-in-the-wall secondhand bookstores.

Leo Rosten's Treasury of Jewish Quotations and The Wordsworth Dictionary of Film Quotations (complied by Tony Crawley) are two volumes just as well-thumbed by their previous owner as they are by us.

Even if your reference is obscure, quotations often provide interesting openings.

> *What is there more kindly than the feeling between host and guest?*
>
> Aeschylus: The Libation Bearers, 458 BC

This quotation from an ancient writer and traveler was the opening Susan used for a hotel review about Windmill Inns of America and its expansion into the luxury suites market. Its goal was to create a feeling of being a guest in someone's home. The introduction of a "host" rather than a frontdesk clerk helped set the right tone for the article.

2. Use a take-off of a well-known expression or saying

There's an old joke that writers should "avoid clichés like the plague." But for that rare comic who can twist words, sayings and clichés can yield some clever, unusual openings.

One example from an unknown author says:

> *Money can't buy you happiness, but on the island paradise of St. Martin it can help rent you some.*

Here's one from a student with a quick wit and a love of race cars:

> *Most people would give their eye teeth to drive a*
> *formula racing car. Tell them to keep their teeth.*

The article went on to describe a brand-new facility where visitors and locals could experience firsthand the adrenaline rush of being behind the wheel of a race car.

As effective as take-off opens can be, they can also be deadly. Be sure it really is funny before you use it. The best acid test we've ever found is to read it to a casual acquaintance; close friends and family tend to be too concerned about not hurting your feelings to be completely honest. If the acquaintance laughs, use it. If he or she gives you a pained expression and forces out a grunt, head back to the computer.

3. Invite your readers to share your version of a universal experience

"Commuting. I confess, I can't stand it. Lineups, layovers, and the dreaded 'UFDs' — unavoidable flight delays." Most people can relate on some level to the misery and perils of commuting, so Susan used this as the opening for a review of a small, Pacific Northwest commuter airline. Even though the article was about how none of these applied to this airline, the opening gave readers the feeling they were being invited to share common experience with the author.

4. Story (anecdote) lead

Story (anecdote) leads often make for strong openings. Can you think of any fishing enthusiast who, after returning from a weekend adventure to "one of the great fishing secrets of the Northern Hemisphere," doesn't tell at least one good, tall fish tale? Probably not.

Storytelling is part of human heritage, and travel writing can, and should, blend all details and descriptions of a particular destination with the creativity of storytelling.

5. Personify the main focus of your story

> *She stood before me, wings outstretched in warm*
> *greeting. Her plexiglass nose seemed to smile her*
> *pleasure at meeting me. "I'm glad you have come,"*
> *she seemed to be saying. "It is good to see you."*
>
> Manuel Erickson

The "she" referred to is a World War II Lancaster bomber that now lives permanently in the Lancaster Museum located in Nanton, Alberta. The article continued on to discuss the history of the museum and its famous leading lady, as well as the community spirit and dedication of the Nanton volunteers.

Personify the main focus of your story to draw in readers.

6. Ask a question

What do glaciers, English high tea, and an art auction have in common?

The purpose of a question lead is to lure the reader (and hopefully the editor who will decide to buy your work) onward into the body of the article. A good question lead is one that immediately involves the reader in the outcome of the story. Make the reader believe the only way to discover the answer is by making time to read the material in front of them: your article.

There is, however, one major danger to this type of lead. It's often a great temptation to pose a question so that the answer is either yes or no:

Ever wonder what glaciers, English high tea, and an art auction have in common?

Worse yet:

Glaciers, English high tea, and an art auction have something in common. Can you guess what it is?

If you use a question lead, be sure the answer is more than a "yes" or a "no."

Not only are these usually flat, uninteresting questions, there is a very real danger that a reader, or an editor, will respond "No, and I don't really care." If you use this type of lead, aim for open-ended questions that create thought-provoking responses in your audience rather than a monosyllabic reply.

Note: So just what *do* glaciers, English high tea, and an art auction have in common? Answer: they can all be found on board Holland America Line's sumptuous cruises through the Inside Passage to Alaska.

Leads, whatever format you decide on, must intrigue your audience. Go for the dramatic, the sensual, or the quirky. Pick that one truly unique aspect of your travel tale, and bait your hook firmly. Then get set to keep reeling them in.

c. The middle

We once heard of an informal study that claimed most novice writers spend approximately 80% of their time working on the middle of a writing project. The remaining 20% was split roughly half and half between the beginning and the ending.

On the surface, this makes sense. After all, the middle is the main course, the "meat and potatoes" of an article (or as one politically correct and vegetarian writer pointed out, the rice and tofu): facts and figures, any quotes you want to include, how to get there, what happened to you when you were there, historical data, and just how many hours you *can* lie in the Hawaiian sunshine without burning — in short, all the relevant details. Naturally, you'd want to spend most of your time working on this section.

However, the same study revealed the majority of experienced writers reverse those percentages. Why? Because if you've done your job with a strong hook, your audience will usually continue reading the rest of your tale no matter what. But here are some noteworthy exceptions:

(a) Poor writing. The greatest hook in the world won't hold a reader through pages of sloppy writing.

(b) Misleading lead. You've mislead the reader into expecting a different type of article or travel tale. (Remember the story about the salmon barbecue and the tulip fields?)

(c) Inaccuracies. Mistakes, even when they are honest ones, have a nasty habit of being remembered by the less forgiving. Rule of thumb: if you don't know for sure, either research until you are sure, or leave it out altogether.

(d) Superficiality. This may have been much prized by the pompous Miss Gwendolen Fairfax in *The Importance of Being Earnest*, but it's fatal to a travel writer.

(e) Off beat presentation and/or grammar. True, Jack Kerouac and e.e. cummings were able to flaunt their unusual style in the face of grammatical rules and get away with it. But until you're at least as well known as they are, stick with normal, everyday punctuation, sentence structure, and paragraph format. There's a lot of truth in the old adage that claims you have to know what the rules are before you can afford to break them with impunity.

Consider the market for your article as you write. The writing style of newspaper articles tends to be more abbreviated than that of their magazine cousins. Short paragraphs and sentences predominate.

It's important to be aware of and use an editor's preferences in terms of style or slant whenever you submit an article to either magazines or newspapers.

If you launch some of your writing into cyberspace via the Internet, you will likely get prompt feedback. Some of it can be helpful in honing your writing skills.

However, before you start thinking you can afford to dash off the middle 1,000 words of your 1,200-word article on the joys of skiing at Aspen or windsurfing at Waikiki, here are some points to remember.

1. Less is often more

It happens in almost every travel writing class. Someone in the group turns out to be a world traveler brimming with enough incredible stories and tales of adventure that Scheharazade would have found herself with some very stiff competition for the sultan's attention.

No matter where your travels take you, the temptation to include every detail, every adventure, every hotel, beach, and marketplace is almost irresistible. After all, you're a travel writer and you want to share ALL those marvelous experiences with your readers. Isn't that what travel writing is all about?

Well, yes . . . and no.

Although we've searched, we have yet to meet a travel writer (or any other writer for that matter) who could cram everything about a three-week trek across South America into 1,000 or 1,500 words.

One student actually tried this. By the time she had reached the end of her second, double-spaced page, she had described her harrowing arrival at the airport, the first night's hotel accommodation that almost wasn't, meals and snacks for the first three days, a shopping expedition at the local marketplace, and was already on a fast track to what could have been a hilarious (and very saleable) story about her misadventures traveling across the mountains aboard one of the local buses.

Give each part of a trip the attention it deserves in your writing. Don't try to cram three weeks into a thousand words.

The writer tantalized us with a few sentences about sharing a seat with a crate of chickens and their owner, a rotund woman wearing enough jewelry to open a small shop and a laugh that stretched from one side of the country to the other. She painted a brief, colorful word picture of careening around hair-pin corners, flanked on one side by stone cliffs climbing to the skies and on the other by a precipice plunging hundreds of feet to a raging river.

Then, without warning, she moved on to a new, totally unrelated, subject: a picnic at her next destination. At that point, readers would do what most editors would do: groan, throw the manuscript to one side, and go on to other stories that didn't drag them into another world, only to dump them before completing the tale.

This writer had a real flair for description, but every time she started delving below the surface of her subject, she moved on to a new one. She had not yet realized that some events and memories simply need to be shared with readers in a different story at another time.

2. Focus

Focus, a close relative of "less is more," is every bit as important to a writer as it is to a visual artist. If you've ever tried to watch an out-of-focus movie, you know how frustrating it can be. Is the riverside seduction taking place along the Thames or the St. Lawrence Seaway? And is that the Empire State Building or just another highrise in an unknown city?

Fuzzy focus will leave your readers confused, irritated, and ready to flip the page the next time they see an article sporting your byline. Let's look at an example:

> *Nevada is one of the few places easily accessible to North Americans where gambling is legal. Much of the state is desert, although the Lake Tahoe area offers exceptional skiing, both cross-country and downhill. Access is easy by either road or air, and many bus tour companies run regular Reno and Las Vegas junkets year-round for those afflicted with a passion for cards and dice. Many musical entertainers and comedians love to perform in these two cities. Las Vegas is also considered to be the hot spot for magicians. For many years, Reno was home to one of the greatest vintage auto collections on the continent — the world renowned Harrah's Auto Collection.*

It's fairly easy to see that this article is going to be about the state of Nevada. It's probably also safe to assume it will talk primarily about Reno and Las Vegas. But what is the focus? Pick your choice:

(a) Getting there

(b) Gambling

(c) Entertainment, such as magic or musicals

(d) Other attractions, such as the car collection

(e) Skiing and other winter sports

Each of these is referred to, but no focus has been defined. Now let's look at the same paragraph after some rewriting.

Psst! Feeling lucky? Figure your hunches are more reliable than the bank rate? Ask any wanna-be card shark and they'll confirm it — Reno and Las Vegas are two of the favorite hot spots for people with a passion for cards and dice. Tour operators have capitalized on the dream of "hitting the jackpot" for decades. By air or by ground, gambling junkets tailored to every imaginable age and interest group are readily available, year-round.

In this example, it's fairly safe to assume the main focus will be the gambling itself. The article will likely present information covering junkets, types of gambling available, and how to get there, and details on specific tours just for gamblers.

Now, how about a different view.

Jackpot! Lights flash. Bells clang. Another gambler's dream comes true as a stream of coins pour from the bowels of a "one armed bandit." But the lure of easy-flowing gold dust isn't limited to those sipping martinis and nibbling caviar around the gaming tables in Reno and Las Vegas. A steady stream of world class musicians, comedians, and entertainers vie for the opportunity and generous returns of playing nightly to packed houses. Illusionists now consider Las Vegas to be the North American "Mecca of Magic," much to the delight of visitors, young and old.

Here the focus has shifted. Gambling, while still important, has taken a backseat to the entertainment available. And we haven't even touched on outdoor sports or the vintage cars! Those are two more articles waiting to be written.

3. Building bridges — not just for bricklayers

Much the same as a bridge leads a traveler comfortably from one riverbank to the other, written bridges provide easy passage from one paragraph or subject to the next. They can be a sentence or only a few words, but in spite of a growing belief that written bridges are no longer necessary, without them your stories will sound choppy and harsh.

Here's an example from Susan's ship review of Holland America Line's *ms Nieuw Amsterdam*.

> *A quick glance through the "Day at a Glance" bulletin assured me life aboard this grand lady of the Holland America Line would be an endless smorgasbord of indulgences for body and spirit. Massage, aerobics, ping pong, glacier watching, an art auction — where to begin?*
>
> *I decided to consider the question over afternoon tea in the Explorer's Lounge. Feeling oh-so-very-British, I sipped orange pekoe, nibbled delicately on crustless cucumber sandwiches, and admired the enormous oil painting of an ancient sea battle. Worldly cares seemed as far away as those billowing white sails.*

The second paragraph could have begun: *One of my favorite activities was afternoon tea in the Explorer's Lounge.* This would technically have served as a bridge between the general list and a specific activity. But by adding only one extra word to the total count, a more lyrical, luxurious feeling that amplified the elegance associated with cruising was created. The writer was about to be so pampered, she could afford to take time to do nothing more than contemplate the choice of leisure activities.

4. Subject hopping

Although too many different subjects create confusion and superficiality, few travel tales contain only one aspect of a destination or attraction.

Let's consider a piece on Disneyland. No trip to the Magic Kingdom is complete without some reference to the rides, but you want your article to have a more unusual slant. You've done a brainstorming web and decided to concentrate on the restaurants, shops, and wandering street entertainment.

Use colored highlighter pens to help you determine if you should write more than one article.

As you re-read your masterpiece, you get an uneasy sense of being out of focus, in spite of painstaking attention to include only your three chosen subjects. The problem may be subject hopping. Perhaps you've started with the shops, gone on to restaurants, back to shopping, briefly discussed the minstrel outside the shop, gone back into

Keep your most exciting, most specific information at the front of an article or chapter unless you are writing in chronological order.

another restaurant, followed by more shopping, and wrapped up with more street entertainment.

A simple, effective method of seeing this problem is as near as a package of highlighters. First, take a yellow highlighter and mark everywhere you've referred to restaurants. Now mark all the shopping information in green, and color every instance of street entertainment in pink. Finally, take a blue highlighter for miscellaneous subjects.

Most well-written articles tend to display colors grouped together. If you're left with a frenzy of color that reminds you of the way your stomach felt as you stepped out of Space Mountain, you need to do some restructuring. Try breaking down each section, especially if you are working on a travel book. Really *look* at what you want to say about each subject. You can always combine sections later.

d. The ending

1. Summing up

Like a good play or symphony, the best endings leave a reader satisfied, yet longing for an encore.

Summing up what was described is one commonly used and effective form of ending. Here's how one writer used this method to conclude a nostalgic look at an early 1970s visit to Russia.

> *I remember caviar lunches and dancing bears playing hockey at the Bolshoi Theatre on ice, the beauty of the Moscow subway, the cleanest and most ornate in the world, the Sputnik Hotel where the water was rarely on and the toilet paper was like sandpaper. I remember thinking...that some day I would like to return to Russia when the country is free. Perhaps I will have to be content cherishing my memories.*
>
> Ann Westlake

2. The circular ending

Another ending style, and one of our favorites, is the circular ending. If you guessed this means referring back to something in the body of the article, give yourself a pat on the back. You're right.

The ship review of the *ms Nieuw Amsterdam* you read earlier has a circular ending. This piece opened with a scene about the chandeliers in the main dining room. Shortly after that, the ship's Passport to Fitness program, where passengers could participate in a fitness program and gain points toward a sweatshirt, was discussed. The review closed with this:

> *Then I remembered the chandeliers. "Pamper yourself," they'd said. Perhaps, in the end, I would just sit back, enjoy the impeccable service, and watch the majestic beauty of Alaska unfold before me.*
>
> *And the sweatshirt? Who knows — maybe next cruise.*

Aim to leave your readers with a sense of having just shared a mini-vacation with you. In no time you'll find you have an audience who can't wait to hear about your next travel adventure.

5
Photo finish

If you are one of those people whose mother won't answer the door when you go calling with your travel photos in hand, this chapter is for you.

If you aspire to publication in glossy magazines such as *National Geographic* or you've taken even one elementary photography course, you can probably skip most of this quick-and-dirty section. Professional photographers, aficionados, and other fanatics will likely cringe at the some of the advice here — but for the photographically challenged, it works.

Why should a travel writer want to learn this skill? Because travel articles will be much more saleable if they are accompanied by reasonable-quality pictures. To mangle a cliché, you can tell a 1,500-word story in 500 words if you have an evocative picture to go along with it.

The key point to take away from this chapter is that you can take travel photos without spending years perfecting the craft of becoming a photographer. Even if you do not get paid specifically for the photos, if your travel articles sell better, you're one step farther down the road to being a travel writer.

In many travel stories, it's common to find photos taking up more space than the words. Editors know readers can be enticed to glance through dry statistics when a sizzling snapshot has already captured their attention. The implied promise is that if readers just read the bit on how to get a cheaper air flight, that beach scene may be within their grasp.

Every photo should tell the reader something about the destination and its people. Depending on the market, the photo doesn't even have to be brilliantly composed or even perfectly focused to tell its own story. As an example, badly focused, grainy pictures of a flaming aircraft, taken from awkward angles, convey the terror of an air crash without having any technical merit at all. Photos like these sometimes sell entire newspapers and magazine issues!

While most of your photos won't have that kind of impact, if you follow this advice, you won't commit the sin of boring your audience either. Publishable photos really require only two things: some technical expertise and reasonable composition.

You can purchase just about all the technical know-how you need right in the camera. We'll show you how later in this chapter.

Good composition, on the other hand, is one of those intangibles that you know when you see, but is often hard to explain. But take heart, with practice and some attention to how other people's published work looks, you can develop a feel for good composition in a surprisingly short time. There are numerous books on photography available at any library. Spend a few hours studying them — the investment will pay off in short order.

The best part is that the practice is fun. Getting out there and using your camera is the easiest and most effective way to improve your photos. It costs a little for film and processing, but if you pay attention to what works and what doesn't, eventually you'll find your photographic stories becoming more and more memorable. And when your mother invites you over to show her some travel shots, you'll know the lessons are paying off!

a. Your first and only technical lesson

The syllabus for your first and only technical lesson is a bit abbreviated, but if you follow its secrets to the letter, you will be a technical expert. No shot will be out of focus, underexposed, or washed out by too much sunlight.

Step one: Go to the nearest camera store and buy a fully automatic camera. Auto flash, auto focus, auto film advance — auto everything. Automatic is a word the photographically challenged have come to love.

Sure, if you want to play with depth of field and f-stops you should be able to switch to manual mode, but with rare exceptions, you hardly ever need adjust the settings to capture great shots. In fact, if you aren't asking what f-stops are, you should be skipping on down to the section on selling your pictures.

Step two? There is no second step. With a modern camera, you are technically as good as many of the photographers published today.

Shocking, yes. But you'd be amazed at the number of travel photos taken with the cheapest automatic cameras.

Such cameras are not without limitations. Shooting just about anything except subjects eight or ten feet away means you lose all but the gross details. The good news is that you'll probably seldom need panoramic shots for publication. Even if you do, there are dedicated inexpensive cameras that do panoramas almost as well as their more expensive counterparts.

b. Features to die for

We are big fans of an indicator showing whether or not there is film in the camera. Most older cameras have a frame counter, but on some models it's hard to tell at the beginning of a roll whether the camera is empty or whether you just haven't advanced the film yet. Make it a habit to always advance the film to the first frame as soon as you load the camera.

With many modern auto-everything cameras, the shutter will not work unless the camera is loaded. A great feature. You did remember to pack film didn't you?

So just what do all the automatic features mentioned above do? Auto focus lets you know ahead of time that every picture you shoot will be sharp. Auto exposure means every image will be correctly exposed. Auto flash means you won't have to make decisions about lighting in dim surroundings — the camera does it for you. Auto wind allows you to take several pictures of a rapidly changing scene without removing your eye from the viewfinder. As well, many auto cameras also feature auto load so when your last picture on the roll is taken, the camera auto rewinds too.

These features may seem like costly "bells and whistles," but in a one-chance-only situation they can mean the difference between taking home a photo or just a memory.

Once in Australia, when a little girl stuck her finger up the nose of a kangaroo at a petting zoo, Rick managed to be in the right place with his camera ready. Snap! A *Life Magazine* back cover for sure. But the next second while he was manually advancing the film, the little girl turned toward the camera, and still holding her finger in the dazed kanga's nose, flashed a bedazzling smile right into the lens. Rick missed it.

When Rick finally had his prize photo developed, it was slightly out of focus and very dark. He had saved a hundred dollars by using an old manual camera and succeeded in losing his retirement jackpot.

On another occasion, he got involved in shooting a skier doing some spectacular death-defying somersaults, only to find afterward that the camera had no film in it. The skier was not the good-natured sport he hoped and refused to do the stunt again.

c. Don't shop 'till you drop

Whether you are talking about an inexpensive pocket camera or a SLR (single lens reflex) with a variety of interchangeable lenses, there are at least a dozen camera brands to choose from.

When we finally investigated upgrading from our Canon Sureshot, we spent months reviewing dozens of different cameras — a whole new field with a lot of technical concepts and its own jargon.

In the end, we realized that all brand name cameras are just about the same. That's right. Any brand name camera will let you take good photos. Today's cameras and lenses are made by computer, so unless you are considering a camera costing under $20, any one of them will give you sharp, properly exposed images.

After a while you'll probably find you prefer certain features of one camera over another. These are things you learn from experience, not by talking with photostore clerks (no matter how knowledgeable) or by aiming the camera around the inside of the store for a few minutes. If you have time and enjoy learning a new skill — great. If your main interest is shooting pictures so you can sell more articles, look for the most comfortable to use, fully automatic camera in the price range you can afford, and buy it.

You can get relatively new brand name cameras repaired in almost any major center in the world within a reasonable time. Technicians will be familiar with them and parts may be right on the shelf: no week-long wait to have the needed part shipped.

There is also a ready secondhand market. Not only can you save some cash when you buy your first camera, but when you are ready to upgrade, you can sell your "old faithful" and recover some of the cost of the new camera. But just like buying a used car, it's smart to take along a knowledgeable friend and be wary of high-pressure salespersons.

1. Moving to jets

(a) Single lens reflex (SLR)

After using a simple point-and-shoot camera for years, we thought the viewfinder of a single lens reflex (SLR) camera was like looking at the instrument panel of a jet. The Canon Sureshot didn't have all those dials and indicators. And with the zoom lens, we could take recognizable pictures of fawns from a distance. Wow! Had to have one of these. No more sneaking up and startling animals and people.

With careful shopping we discovered that a more-than-adequate SLR camera with lens can be had for somewhere between $500 and $800 new — much less secondhand. Technology has become so good that even cheap SLR cameras with interchangeable lenses will produce images suitable for newspapers and many magazines.

(b) Advanced photo system (APS)

APS stands for advanced photo system. You may be tempted to consider an APS camera, which looks a lot like a 35mm camera. But APS uses a different, narrower film than 35mm — 24mm to be exact. You'll likely have to fight off salespeople assuring you an APS is better than a 35mm. It probably is. But if you ever hope to sell your photos to the big glossy magazines, keep in mind that they almost certainly won't have the special computer-controlled equipment to deal with the new size negative used by APS cameras. At least not yet. And depending on several factors — quality and cost being only two — magazines may never adopt the format. After all, it took more than a quarter of a century for the publishing industry to accept 35mm rather than their larger format predecessors.

If you want to sell your photos as prints only, this new system is worth considering when you trade up in the next few years. At the moment, however, the process is too new, which means it's not as widely available as 35mm color negative processing (the ubiquitous C4 process). You'll probably have to wait much longer than one hour at your local drug store.

(c) Digital cameras

Digital cameras are being sold as the wave of the future, and no doubt about it, they are. But today's digital cameras — at least the one's most of us can afford — are like the spring wound 78 rpm phonograph compared with today's CD. They produce images only marginally clearer than the paused stillframe on your VCR. Experts will tell you they have "640 by 480 resolution" which is correct. But all that means is there are 640 colored dots along each of 480 lines making up the whole picture. Not very many when you consider the average color print from a negative has at least 1,000 by 1,000 color dots every square inch. Put another way, those digital pictures look best when reproduced in a half-inch square.

2. In praise of disposables

Camera bugs may chirp in disgust, but disposable cameras do have their place. Picture quality, while not wonderful, is usually sufficient for most newspapers and many magazines.

There are also specialized disposable cameras. For example, unless you do a lot of underwater work and can afford the big bucks to purchase or rent an underwater camera, the disposable underwater cameras are a very cheap alternative. They are good for photos down to a depth of approximately 6 feet (1.83 meters) which is all you need for snorkeling, white water rafting, or swimming and boating shots.

Disposable cameras also make cheap backups for your normal battery-sucking, relatively fragile, main camera. Waiting for sunrise at the edge of a volcanic crater that took most of the night to reach is not the time to find out you have a malfunctioning camera and no backup. (Not that this ever happened to any of us, of course.)

Disposable cameras are often used as a kind of currency. Barbara was shocked at the number of tourists who did not take a camera of any kind to the Great Barrier Reef in Australia. The boat crew on a tour she took produced a bag full of disposable cameras, which were generously offered to the passengers for about twice the going rate at the pier. There were several takers.

In really desperate circumstances, disposables can be worth much more. Rick graciously gave away his backup disposable to an unfortunate person whose camera died in the middle of a 38-foot (12-meter) yacht race with some America's Cup sailors — a once in a lifetime opportunity. Later that evening, a bottle of very good champagne was delivered to his room.

d. The right lens

Camera lenses come in three basic varieties: short, regular, and long; also known as wide-angle, normal, and telephoto. Lenses are specified in millimeters focal length. You can tell the difference between them first by their sizes. The wide-angle is short, the telephoto is long, and the normal lens somewhere in between. There is a fourth variety, and one which we recommend. It combines various features of the other lenses. It is the zoom lens and is by far the most versatile.

Some disposable cameras have panoramic lens capability that allows you to shoot a double-wide picture. This is a terrific feature and a cheaper solution than adding an expensive and difficult-to-find regular panoramic camera to your gear.

Disposable cameras are great if you are worried about theft. In some places, having a good camera is like hanging a bar of gold around your neck — not something you want to do in Rio at night.

Tailor your equipment to the particular terrain you're visiting Don't bother with telephoto lenses if you're in dense forest, for example; the light will be too dim and nothing will be sufficiently far away to warrant lugging them along.

Similarly, forget the wide-angle lens out on the big-sky prairie or desert unless you have a need for a picture of miles and miles of very little except sky.

All short, wide-angle lenses distort the image somewhat. The shorter the lens, the more distortion, particularly in vertical structures such as buildings. Very short lenses curve every straight line. The shortest lenses, called fish-eye, are characterized by profound distortion of their 180° view.

Every SLR camera manufacturer has one of these in its catalogue, but generic varieties are usually less expensive, without noticeable quality difference. Secondhand they're cheaper still.

Even if you are using a wide-angle lens, you will still need to take care when photographing tall buildings; even a modest tilt up from the horizontal causes buildings to "lean back."

Telephoto lenses tend to be heavy. If you're using anything longer than 200mm, you'll definitely need a tripod.

1. The wide-angle lens

Short focal length lenses, less than 50mm, are called wide-angle because they encompass a wider field of view than the normal lens. They also make images that exaggerate the distance of things from the camera, like those curved rear-view mirrors that make objects look farther away. The shorter the focal length, the more exaggerated that effect.

The wide-angle lens is used when you need to get as much of a view into one image as possible or when you can't back up enough to include everything.

The best wide-angle lens to buy is a 28mm. These are good, moderately short lenses that gives a wide field of view without excessive distortion.

2. The normal lens

The normal lens for a 35mm camera is 50mm focal length. Why? Because it gives an image on the film that looks just like the image you see with your eye.

This is the lens that used to come with a new camera when you bought it. Pictures taken with a normal lens look correct to the eye. You can also take pictures with less light using this lens than with any of the other lenses. At one time, if you could afford only one lens, this was the one to have. However it has now been superseded by the 35mm to 70mm zoom lens.

3. The telephoto lens

Long focal length lenses, more than 50mm, act like telescopes and take in a smaller field of view than the 50mm lens, depending on their focal length. The longer the lens, the more telescopic its effect.

Telephoto lenses allow you to stand well back from the intake end of animals and machinery and still get the shot. You can drag an image out of the background that would be lost using any shorter lens because, much like using a pair of binoculars, you're photographing only a small section of the view in front of you.

The disadvantage is that telephotos need more light than do most other lenses, so in dim light, exposure times are increased. As well, the longer the lens, the more difficult it is to hold it steady. When these two problems combine, they usually result in blurred pictures.

4. The zoom lens

If you can afford only one lens, go for a zoom. The zoom replaces a whole series of lenses.

Experts will tell you that an assortment of the first three lenses will give you sharper photos than a zoom. Maybe. This advice reminds us of our first stereo systems. The salespeople talked us into much higher-priced systems because the sound quality was so much better. Frankly, Led Zeppelin sounded just fine on a cheaper system to us. Grainy newspaper reproduction doesn't get worse just because you used a zoom lens instead of the exact lens a professional might use. Today, even modestly priced zoom lenses outperform yesterday's models.

Choose the 35mm to 70mm zoom (or a 30mm to 80mm if you can get it). This lens is the best all-round bet, and you don't need to fiddle about changing it for every shot. They rival yesterday's normal lenses in sharpness and image quality at all settings, from wide (35mm) to long (70mm).

As well, most of these new, computer-designed lenses have a macro setting. In other words, they focus closer than other lenses, and at full zoom this means very close.

Just about every new SLR camera is sold with a version of this zoom as its prime lens, and for good reason. It combines versatility in a package hardly larger or heavier than a normal 50mm lens.

Disadvantages of the 35mm to 70mm zoom lens are few, if any. For the very picky person who wants to use the slowest film, the lens needs a bit more light than a normal 50mm lens. But if you use our recommended choice of 200 ASA color film, you will never notice.

Zoom lenses are wonderful for composing a picture without having to move. Just zoom in and out to include different parts of the scene.

Your 35mm to 70mm zoom should normally live on the camera. It is the most versatile lens, particularly when that once-in-a-lifetime shot pops up. It is a people lens, indoors and out, ideal for city and beach, cruise liner or train; ideal, in fact, for most travel situations.

At the very least, fit every lens you own with a cheap UV filter. It will improve blue sky contrast and also protect your valuable lenses from damaging dust, mud, and salt. As well, it's cheaper to replace a scratched UV filter ($10 to $15) than your expensive lens any day.

e. Filters

Dozens of filters are on the market that do everything from polarizing light to darkening one half of the picture.

All you really need is a polarizing filter. Those glossy travel-magazine pictures of incredibly white sand with a deep turquoise ocean in the background are the work of the polarizing filter. It cuts down glare and increases the contrast in brilliantly sunlit scenes. This is really useful at the beach or anywhere you are shooting a very bright blue sky or dazzling reflections.

Some people rave about the vibrant yellows of one brand of film or the scintillating blues of another. It's true there are subtle differences between films, and you will probably develop preferences depending on what you like to shoot. Land and seascapes benefit from more vibrant blues and greens, while people shots look better with brighter yellows. Try different brand names to see what you prefer.

It pays to buy brand name film such as Fuji or Kodak. You can get it anywhere in the world, you can be sure of the quality, and it's easy to have processed.

Unfortunately, it is one of the most expensive filters on the market. And you'll need one for each lens unless your lenses happen to be all of the same diameter. Still, a polarizing lens works miracles in bright outdoor settings.

f. Film

Never shoot with black-and-white film. Not only is it harder to find someone to develop it, you'll also want the option of selling the photo to color magazines, and increasingly, color newspapers. Besides, black and whites can be made from color film, but without a good set of crayons, it's difficult to do it the other way around.

Some editors want color slides to work with. Others want prints. You need to know this before you purchase your film, since slide film is different from print film. It is possible to make slides from print film and vice versa, but the quality suffers dramatically and it is expensive.

If you are writing for a particular magazine, the submission guidelines will tell you which it prefers. If there are no specific guidelines, stick with prints. Prints are easier to handle, cheap to duplicate, and you don't need a projector or light table to examine them.

We recommend using 200 ASA color film. 100 ASA will certainly do, but 200 ASA allows you to shoot indoors, at twilight, and on dark and rainy days with better results.

We generally have our film developed after returning from a trip. You will find that it is easier to transport as undeveloped film, and if there is a problem or delay in processing, you won't be left wondering how to pick up the pictures the next afternoon when your flight home leaves the city that evening. However, some countries may refuse to allow you to carry undeveloped film out of the country for military or other security reasons, so you should check ahead of time.

Some companies sell discounted, no-name brands of film at bargain prices, but you usually have to send your film by mail to another city for processing. The savings are not worth the worry of losing your prize pictures in the mail, or the hassle of writing to find out if they were received by the lab in the first place — assuming you made a note of the lab's address. Don't take a chance: forget this type of film altogether.

One-hour processing outlets have improved dramatically over the past few years. We have had spotty luck with them in the past, but even local supermarket labs turn out excellent negatives these days. Most cities also have several good custom labs. Ask around for a recommendation. A good lab should be able to correct minor exposure problems with your negatives by custom printing, hence their name. (Some can even take people out of a photo by digitizing it and using a nifty computer program.)

Keep all your negatives and prints in a clean, dust- and moisture-free place that is not exposed to excesses of heat or cold. Negatives are best kept in an album with specially designed negative sleeves so that, like prints, you can see what they are without fear of fingerprints or other handling marks. Sunlight fades colors, so avoid leaving negatives or prints where the sun might shine directly on them (e.g., on a windowsill). Treat negs and prints like the valuable investment they are.

g. Camera protection

Protecting your camera should be an ever-present thought while you are traveling. Here are some suggestions:

- Buy insurance for your camera in case of loss or damage.

- Always pack your camera with your carry-on luggage at the airport. Never check it in with the cargo luggage.

- The safest place for your camera is around your neck; the new generation of cameras can be hung there without giving you a permanent hunch.

- Consider a Pelican Box on any trip involving water. These are strong plastic, waterproof cases lined with foam rubber. The big advantage is that the box opens along its long axis like a pelican's beak. Everything in the box is easily accessible.

  Most come with a quick release fastener so you can lift your equipment (or candy bar) out quickly. You can also easily drill small holes in some of the outside hinges and flanges. (Not in the side of the case — you'll lose the water proofing.) This enables you to tie the box down to a kayak or boat deck but still open the lid quickly.

  The biggest disadvantage is that these boxes are a dead give-away that you are carrying photo equipment, and probably high-quality equipment. Nimble-fingered thieves are

In many countries, film is two to three times as expensive as it is in the United States and Canada. Hotels are notorious for charging outrageous prices, and walking the streets looking for cheap film in a strange place is never fun, so stock up with more film than you could conceivably want before you leave home. You'll need it. We average one roll of 36 exposures per day on a busy sightseeing tour.

Film lasts for years if it is kept in the refrigerator, so don't feel it will be wasted if you have a few rolls left over at the end of your trip. Make sure to enclose it in a tightly sealed plastic box or polybag. When using it again, take it out of the refrigerator to warm up for several hours before opening the box. This prevents condensation problems.

Never use outdated film for anything important. The natural background radiation (harmless to us) changes colors and fogs unexposed film over time.

constantly on the lookout for signals of an easy mark like this. You'll need to be even more aware of your camera at all times.

- Register your camera equipment with customs before you leave the country. The few minutes it takes will avoid any possibility of it being confiscated as undeclared contraband when you return. There is no insurance for confiscated cameras.

h. Before you leave home, and on the road

Make sure your camera works before you leave home with it. If you haven't used it in a while, shoot a roll of film to make sure; be sure to take flash pictures too. Trying to figure out what's wrong with your camera on the road can ruin a fun day. Finding out after you get home that your camera wasn't working is even worse.

Most cameras are too complicated for you to repair by the side of the road. Still, it is worth carrying a small repair kit with your camera. The emphasis should be on small. A basic repair kit includes —

- Super glue
- A few inches of duct tape
- A selection of suitable screwdrivers
- A small air brush for removing dust from the lens. This looks like a small turkey baster with a flexible bulb that you can squeeze to force air through a tube — great for removing dust from fragile places.
- Silica gel packs to keep your equipment dry in humid places
- Spare, fresh batteries
- Your owner's manual

A word of warning: Tiny screwdriver sets are sold by the millions and are sometimes as cheap as a buck. Camera stores will sell everything you need, but at far higher prices. Before you leave home, check that the screwdrivers fit the screws on your camera. Some cameras require a special screwdriver which looks like a normal Phillips driver but is not. Using the wrong driver can create a real problem if you ruin the head of a screw.

i. The perfect picture

Composing a picture is the fun part of photography. The best way to learn composition is to go out and shoot pictures. Don't be afraid to waste film. Analyze your results, see how they stack up against pictures published in the glossy magazines. There really is no other way to learn the art.

Here are some suggestions which will help develop your inner eye:

1. Does this picture tell a story?

Imagine a cutline (caption) for the pictures you are taking. "Tinkersville is so poor that the starving dogs all look like draped flour sacks." And, of course, the picture is of a pitiful-looking creature all floppy skin and sad eyes.

The caption test is a good tip off that the photo may be unremarkable. If you can't think of an exciting cutline, the photo is probably boring.

2. Does this picture evoke an emotion?

People relate to other people in photos. If your article is about the love affairs in and around a county's bridges, a photo of fall leaves on a bridge deck might add a poignant dimension to the theme of your story.

A common type of travel picture is the close-up of a bevy of happy, contented faces. It may be cliché, but it turns up frequently because it shows the reader that this is a marvelous place for a vacation.

3. Does this picture show something unique or unusual about the destination?

One of the prime uses of a travel photo is to show the reader something out of the ordinary. Pick what you think is unique about a place. Just be careful you don't pick something so "unique" that it has already appeared in a hundred other travel articles.

Look for the unlikely. People are fascinated by unusual rock formations or ugly animals. These photos can be an arresting complement to your story.

4. How about people and animals?

People and animals are a safe bet as subjects for your photos. Put action in your shots by including people doing things; it gives the reader something to relate to. Drinking coffee in an open-air café, riding a horse, swimming, even shopping all draw the reader into the scene. If people are not available, animals can be a good second-best.

However, both species should be treated with a bit of caution, for some have unexpected reactions to cameras, which can make them dangerous. Rick once photographed a beach scene, only to have a nefarious-looking man break his camera for including him in the photo.

The shut-one-eye trick: When you're composing a photograph, shut one eye and look again. If what you see looks flat and uninteresting, that's exactly what you'll get if you photograph it. The reason this trick works is because photos are two dimensional and so is looking at a scene or subject with one eye.

Some cameras and flash units have a feature that triggers the flash several times in the second before the photo is actually taken. The eye has time to react to this prolonged strobe and closes down its iris so the light is not reflected back the same way.

Animals and people also present another peculiar problem known as red eye. If all your relatives at the family reunion look like demons from the *Exorcist,* it might be the camera's fault (or then again, perhaps it is your ancestry).

Seriously though, red eye is caused by the camera's flash reflecting back from the retina of the eye. The eye's iris constricts when faced with overwhelming light, but with the speedy electronic flash there isn't time for it to react. So the film gets an imprint of the entire vein system at the back of the eye.

There are several solutions. Ninety-nine percent of the problem occurs when people are looking directly at the camera lens. Directing them to look slightly away from the camera usually avoids red eye pictures and, as a bonus, encourages a more candid aura to your shots.

5. Have you resisted temptation?

We are not alone in our attempts to imitate Ansel Adams's great landscapes. After many hundreds of dollars worth of wasted film, we learned the First Commandment of Landscape Photography: Stay away from all green-leafed jungle scenes, seascapes, and stunning panoramas.

Avoid the face-in-the-middle-of-the-picture syndrome. You'll waste half the frame on air above the head. And take time to check the background to that smiling visage. A centrally placed face with a telephone pole growing out the back of the head will never sell. It also brands you as a rank amateur.

Try to fill the frame with your subject. We once shot a whole roll of film of eagles with a pocket camera with no special lenses. When developed, the photos were fields of blue sky with tiny dots in the center. Unless your subject fills at least a half of the viewfinder frame, get closer or use a telephoto lens.

The great panorama shot is always a temptation because you want to capture the magnificence you see. The camera, with its narrower field of view, cuts out most of it. Leaves and waves look the same all over the world and once you've seen one . . .

6. Where are the photos going to be published?

When taking pictures to accompany your writing, consider where your photos are most likely to be published. Fine detail is often lost in newspaper reproductions, so get close and fill the frame with the subject (use your zoom).

Glossy color magazines require you to take more care to ensure the focus and exposure of the images are perfect. Don't send any that aren't.

Don't shoot pictures that require color for their best effect if you are selling to a black-and-white publication. Sunsets lose their glow in shades of gray.

j. Your safety and your camera

Cameras are fascinating instruments and can become a consuming passion. Concentrating on that tiny image in the viewfinder can blind you to dangers. The "to die for" photo does not exist.

Here is a sampler of compromising and deadly compositions.

(a) It is an old cartoon joke, but it really does happen. We know of a Montréal man who died taking photos of the city from the roof of his house. He kept stepping backward to get a few more buildings in . . .

(b) Unless you have a very good insurance policy on your subjects, do not mindlessly ask them to back up either.

(c) One of the authors (nameless) was brained by a rake when he stepped backward onto the prongs. The camera survived. The photo of the house was blurry.

(d) A riveting close-up of a poisonous snake left one photographer with a couple of interesting indentations in his forehead. As far as we know, no one has gone to retrieve the camera he dropped.

(e) There should be a warning on wide-angle lenses: "Objects may appear farther away than they actually are." Photographing anything moving quickly toward you can be dangerous. Trains, cars, bikes, and nightclub bouncers all seem to reach the end of your lens with surprising speed. Unfortunately, photos of tire treads and tonsils do not sell well.

(f) Cameras are expensive and the natural tendency is to grab them when they fall. Grabbing quickly while at alligator farms or from moving vehicles can disarm any photographer. Look before you reach.

In short, take time to identify dangers and imagine what the worst that could happen might be. Animals (including people), machinery, and high places should heighten your alertness. Know where you are in relation to potential problems.

k. Which photos to send with your article?

If you managed to capture an armed robber on film just as he exited the bank, keep the words in the article to less than 20. You can't do any better. But if your photos are not the central focus of your submission to a publication, pick out the ones you feel:

(a) Supplement the story. One of Rick's stories about a small Mexican village marketplace was accompanied by a picture of a corroded Spanish cannon which two fishermen were trying to sell illegally to a tourist. The story said quaint, crafty, colorful things about the village while the photo added a dimension of skullduggery and mystery.

(b) Underscore a portion of the story or give the reader an accurate view of something too complex to describe in words. Think of Dealey Plaza where J.F. Kennedy was shot and the relationship of the infamous grassy knoll to the School Book Depository. You could use a map and a bunch of words, but a photo from the right place explains it all.

(c) Show the reader how big a ship really is or how old the hotel is.

When you are quite sure about what you want to underscore, select two or three photos to send with an article. Sometimes there are several points to a story, so you may want to send a representative sample of different subjects mentioned in the article and let the editor decide.

It is not unusual to have an editor call and ask if you have more pictures of a particular subject. The editor may have an idea what he or she would like to see but doesn't find it in the specific photos you sent.

Usually, you shouldn't need to send more than a dozen prints. Some writers send contact sheets to save money on postage and prints. This is especially thrifty if you are submitting ideas or queries to several publications at a time.

l. Submitting your photos

Never submit the negatives or the only print you have — especially if you are sending an unsolicited manuscript. If they get lost it doesn't really matter whether it was the publication's or the postal system's fault — they're still gone. One good option is to send color photocopy samples of your work. These are good enough for an editor to decide if your photos are usable, and if they go astray, you're only out the couple of dollars in copying charges.

When you do send photos, write your name and address, some information about the subject, and any appropriate caption on a small square of paper, and tape it to the back of each photo. Do not write directly on the back of a picture. It's all but impossible to press lightly enough so that you don't score the front surface of the picture. Also, ink sometimes smears.

m. Other ways to get photos for your articles

1. Tourist boards and other service-oriented companies

Many tourist boards, airlines, and tour operators have spent thousands of dollars on professional photographs and have developed killer collections. Tahiti Tourism, for instance, hired professionals over a long period to build extensive libraries of every conceivable subject concerning French Polynesia. You want lovable kids/dolphins/sharks eating/swimming/smiling at breakfast/twilight or midnight? They have it.

All these companies want publicity and seldom charge anything for using their photos as long as the article is about them. It is not uncommon to have them pay all shipping charges, which is especially wonderful when you are in a rush to meet a deadline.

Request a press package from the tourist board when you are researching a destination. If there are no photos in the package, ask immediately what kinds of photos are available. Considering you might need to take several rolls of film, plus weeks of waiting for the right light or weather, just to duplicate the shots the tourist board already has, you can see where it pays in time and money to know what they have before you get there. They may also have photos, such as aerial shots, that would cost you a fortune to produce. You can then concentrate your efforts on photos that are unique to your story.

2. Hotels

Hotels are another great source of free photos. Naturally they almost always include pictures of the hotel which you may or may not want

If you want your pictures back, be sure to enclose a self-addressed stamped envelope (SASE). This isn't just because editors aren't willing to bear the cost of returning unused, unsolicited pictures. You don't want to give them any excuse to procrastinate sending back your property. If they can't find a stamp they may put your photos down somewhere among the piles of manuscripts in their office, never to be seen again.

Tourist boards in particular are usually happy to lend or give slides and prints free of charge if they think there is a good chance an article about them will be published.

Even when you are planning extensive photography of an area, make arrangements to see what the tourist board has. More than once our own photos have disappointed us because of camera or operator malfunction. Having a backup set of photos saves a lot of stress when on a tight deadline.

to use, but occasionally the hotel will have a photo that can be used as a general picture of the destination.

Be creative. If your article on the rustic charm of an island has no place for the photo of the ritzy XYZ Hotel, it still might use the hotel's picture of the view from the top floor. The caption might read, "The island's natural beauty is a draw for winter-weary North Americans (photo courtesy of XYZ Hotel)." The hotel is happy and you have a million-dollar shot free for the asking.

3. Photo libraries and CD-ROMs

It used to be that in the old days before 1992, if you wanted a photo of a particular place or a particular subject and you didn't want to send someone out to shoot the picture, you could use a stock-photo library. All you did was reach for the photo library's catalogue on your shelf, thumb through the index, and turn to the appropriate section for dozens of glorious photos of any subject you could imagine.

We do not keep a photo library just "in case" we do an article on that destination one day. It takes too much time to keep it organized, and the photos are often quickly dated.

Do keep photos on hand for any ongoing series. If, for example, you publish several articles on Tahiti each year, keep those photos accessible.

Then you called the stock-photo office to find the price for a one-time or multiple use of a specific picture. Once you paid the price, sometimes several thousand dollars and rarely less than a hundred, you had your image.

With the advent of CD-ROM technology, multitudes of companies, such as Microsoft, are buying up entire libraries and reducing them to digital format. Now you can get several thousand images for $35, with often unlimited free usage.

Using equally cheap programs, you can view these images on your computer, pick the ones you like, and transfer the digitized image to diskette ready for mailing to the publication.

Most publications can deal with this medium, but the technology is new enough that standards are still developing. Be sure you check with the editor about exactly what he or she needs if you are going to use a digital format. And be sure to carefully read your licensing agreement on the CD-ROM wrapper to see what you are allowed to do with the photos. Some licenses allow unlimited use while others are restricted to non-commercial applications only.

n. Getting permission

1. Get permission in writing

Photos and other images are subject to copyright laws. Using a picture without someone's permission is a good way to get your quill, and your bankbook, permanently broken.

To avoid confusion and legal problems later, get all releases *in writing* for each picture you use. Trying to get permission quickly over the phone can be dangerous. Verbal descriptions sometimes work, but too often you may find that you are talking about one photo and the tourist board representative is thinking of another out of its collection. Faxing photos usually helps clarify exactly which picture is being discussed.

Permissions, and the ease of obtaining permissions, vary depending on the photos in question. Since most tourist boards want you to promote them, they are usually happy to give you written permission to use a particular photo. Some CD-ROM manufacturers give blanket permission to the user to use their photos (see above for more detail).

With travel books, publishers will have guidelines outlining what is expected. For instance, they might require you use a standard form that their legal department dreamed up, or they might want to acquire the permissions themselves, and all you need to do is supply the name and address of the copyright holder. Be sure you understand exactly what they want.

Keep track of permissions by stapling a copy of the picture to the release and putting it all in one file.

2. Is the owner of the photograph the copyright holder?

A little more obscure point, but one that travel writers run into frequently — permission from the owner of the photograph doesn't necessarily mean you have permission from the copyright holder. For instance, a hotel may have a picture of the property on the cover of its brochure that they have used for years. The manager, legal beagle that he is, signs a permission statement that says you can use it, no problem. However, there is every chance that the actual copyright holder is the photographer, not the hotel. The photographer may have given permission to the hotel only to use the picture in any brochure, not for publicity. Uh oh.

Sample #2
Standard photo release form

PHOTO RELEASE

Date: _____

I grant _____, and/or his/her legal representatives, the irrevocable right to reproduce the attached photographs. These images may be published for any professional purpose, including advertising. I will hold the above blameless from any liability caused by blurring, distortion, or alteration to the final photograph unless it can be proved the intent of such blurring, distortion, or alteration was to cause malicious damage.

I certify that I am authorized to grant this permission and that I hold the copyright to this material. I further certify that I have read and understand this release and consent to the terms and conditions as defined above.

Name (please print): _____

Address: _____

_____

Signature: _____

Witness: _____

Note: Be sure to check with any publication before you submit photo material to confirm this release is consistent with their guidelines. Some publications may require you to use their own release form before they will accept material from you.

Your photo release form might keep you from losing a legal fight or it might not. Who wants to spend the time and money to find out? Be sure to ask who owns the copyright and who is licensed to grant permissions. Sample #2 shows a standard photo release form; you should use a form such as this before using a photo taken by someone else.

When dealing with small- to medium-sized bureaucracies, it's sometimes difficult to figure out who actually owns the copyright to a photograph. As a rule, the bigger the organization, the easier it is. Large companies can afford an art department which keeps track of who owns what and can quickly tell you if you can have permission to use a photo. In smaller companies, the person who arranged for the company to use the photo may have left without ever documenting fully who owns copyright. Like we have, you can spend a lot of money and time trying to pin it down.

If there is a strong likelihood of your using a particular photo, find out as soon as you can who owns the copyright and what you are allowed to do with it.

3. Photographing people

Several points about photographing people when you travel are worth remembering. It is smart but not always practical to get the permission of the people you are photographing. A friend once took a photo of a man with a dancing bear in Turkey and then faced the choice of a beating or paying $10. The man made his living posing for tourists for cash. Everyone on the street except our friend understood that. Had he asked beforehand he would have been in the know too.

Also, you never know where your photo will end up. It is not unheard of to have the subject of photo recognize themselves in a publication and demand payment as a model. Ideally you want to get a signed release.

Sample #3 shows a model release form. The most important consideration for release forms is what releases the publication requires. Check its guidelines.

If a press release comes with a particular photo, the public relations executive will know all the details about it now, including who owns copyright to the photo, but may not remember anything several months down the road. Find out now who owns copyright.

Sample #3
Model release form

MODEL RELEASE

Date: _____

I grant _____, and/or his/her legal representatives, the irrevocable right to reproduce photographs taken of me on _____(date) at _____. These images may be published for any professional purpose, including advertising. I will hold the above-named photographer blameless from any liability caused by blurring, distortion, or alteration to the final photograph unless it can be proved the intent of such blurring, distortion, or alteration was to cause malicious damage to me. I certify I am over 18 years of age and that I have read and understand the terms of this release.

Name (please print): _____

Address: _____

_____

Signature: _____

Witness: _____

Parental consent (if applicable)

I certify that I am the parent/legal guardian of the minor, _____.
I have read and understand this release and consent to the terms and conditions as defined above.

Name (please print): _____

Address: _____

_____

Signature: _____

Witness: _____

Note: Legal age varies in different parts of the world. Be sure you confirm and have any necessary changes initialled by you, the model, and the model's parent/guardian if necessary.

6
Before, during, and after — develop your game plan

Travel writers can generally be divided into two broad groups: those who write strictly for fun after the fact and those who want to carve a career (whether part time or full time) out of travel writing.

If your goal is to earn a living by selling your travel tales, the preplanning steps in this section will help you maximize any trip's potential. Even if travel writing is more of an enjoyable pastime than a professional calling, use the information here to help you experience and enjoy a destination more fully. Checklist #1 provides a quick reference to keep you on track while you're traveling.

a. Before you go

1. Research your destination

How many steps are there to the top of the Sun Pyramid? Can I drink the water when I get there? How much is Picasso's painting of Don Quixote worth? How long did it take to carve Mount Rushmore?

If you're a historian or have already visited the area you're traveling to many times before, you may have the answers to these types of questions ready to spice up your tale of exploration and wanderlust; but even if you aren't or haven't, there's an easy solution. Read, read, read before arriving at any destination. Cultivate a passionate obsession about the area you're about to visit and research will become a pleasure, not a chore.

Checklist #1
Planning a research trip

BEFORE YOU GO	**TAKE WITH YOU**

BEFORE YOU GO

☐ Research your destination.

☐ Contact tourist bureaus and local attractions.

☐ Research potential article markets.

☐ Get a letter of assignment (see chapter 8).

☐ Send queries to potential sponsors.

☐ Read any media kits your sponsors send to you.

☐ Check out your equipment, such as your camera.

☐ Get any necessary immunization shots.

☐ Get any necessary visas or tourist cards.

☐ Draw up a list of important documents, leaving a copy of everything at home, including:

    ☐ passport number (or leave a copy of the first pages)

    ☐ credit card numbers

    ☐ traveler's checks

TAKE WITH YOU

☐ Useful guide or map books

☐ Journal and a lot of pens

☐ Laptop computer

☐ Story ideas that you will be working on

☐ Appropriate clothing —

    ☐ to wear for meetings

    ☐ relevant to the customs of the country you're visiting

    ☐ comfortable footwear

    ☐ clothing suitable for planned activities (e.g., diving)

☐ Camera

☐ Batteries

☐ Film

☐ Itinerary

☐ Tickets or vouchers

    ☐ airline

    ☐ train

    ☐ cruise

    ☐ theater

    ☐ hotel

☐ Confirmation information for car/hotel/cruise/flight reservations

☐ Valid passport and/or picture identification

☐ Visas or tourist cards

☐ Medical insurance

Checklist #1 — Continued

TAKE WITH YOU
(continued)

- ☐ Driver's license/international driver's permit
- ☐ Credit card necessary for car rental
- ☐ Traveler's checks
- ☐ Foreign currency
- ☐ Business cards
- ☐ Several copies of your bio to leave with people
- ☐ Letter of assignment
- ☐ Copies of recent articles
- ☐ Copy of publication that is printing your article
- ☐ Contact numbers of people you have meetings with
- ☐ Alarm clock
- ☐ Plenty of time to arrive at airport

WHILE YOU'RE AWAY

- ☐ Pick up information on anything you might mention in your article. It will make your job of spelling and verifying names easier later on.
  - ☐ postcards
  - ☐ brochures from local attractions
  - ☐ menus
  - ☐ hotel brochures
  - ☐ business cards from attractions

- ☐ chamber of commerce and tourist bureau publications
- ☐ the local daily (or weekly) newspaper
- ☐ freebie newspapers and magazines
- ☐ Keep copious notes on everything.
- ☐ Meet people you contacted from home.

WHEN YOU GET BACK

- ☐ Write thank-you notes to everyone.
- ☐ Organize your notes and memorabilia.
- ☐ Have your film developed.
- ☐ Send more queries to get your article published.
- ☐ Follow up on pre-trip queries.
- ☐ Write your article.
- ☐ Send a copy of your article to those mentioned in it.

For entertaining and obscure facts, the Guinness Book of World Records, along with a host of other trivia books, is an often-overlooked resource. If you want to add some lighthearted anecdotes to your travel tales, these books can be fun, educational, and provide a great spin-off point for unusual story ideas — like what were the juicy details about the miller's brazen daughter who had an affair with the Lord of the Manor's son in 1567?

A couple of days in the library will reveal a wealth of information about any travel destination. Europe, China, North America, even Antarctica. With minimal effort, you'll discover there are hundreds of excellent source books on popular destinations and almost as many on most of the obscure ones.

To start off your own quest for information, here are some resources to watch for:

- Baedeker publications
- Berlitz's Executive Travel Guides
- Birnbaum guides
- Canadian and American Automobile Association publications
- Fielding's guides
- Fodor's travel guides
- Frommer's Comprehensive Guides
- Michelin guides
- Passport's Illustrated Travel Guides (from Thomas Cook)
- Rick Steves's European travel guides
- Triptiks road map and guide books
- Tourism and tourist bureau publications

Tourism offices, visitors' bureaus, and chambers of commerce are three traditional places to find up-to-the-minute information and tidbits about an area. Radio and TV broadcasts, magazines, and the local daily newspapers are three more, but so are the "freebies" published in most towns and cities. Don't thumb your nose just because they don't cost.

Some writers worry that with all this reading, they may inadvertently copy someone else's writing style and be accused of plagiarism. Rest assured, it doesn't matter how hard you try, it's impossible for your own unique voice to remain silenced.

If a group of writers are told to write about the same city, sure two or three people may pick the same broad subject — let's say the theatrical scene. But where one will concentrate on the latest glitzy musical extravaganza from Broadway, another will look at the small experimental theaters, and a third may concentrate on the cultural influence of First Nations or Inuit drama.

When you're ready for a break from reading, talk to people. Talk to anyone you can think of who's been where you're going —

friends, family, neighbors, coworkers, your weight-training partner at the gym, the crossing guard at the local schoolground. Their recommendations and experiences can often yield invaluable advance insights.

Prior to one of our trips to Puerto Vallarta, someone told us about a small restaurant all but unknown except among the locals and the cruiseline crews. Good thing she also warned us about the half-hidden, gravel driveway and tacky plastic tablecloths or we would have missed out on one of the finest meals of our stay. It was an article waiting to be written: giant shrimp lounging amid red peppers and a dazzling array of exotic spices, full-bodied burgundy, sinfully dark chocolate cake with coffee. And the best part was that this glorious gastronomic extravaganza cost less than $15 per person.

Don't forget about the Internet as a research tool. Our first experience with Internet research was watching a computer guru pick a word (we think it was "fungus") at random from the dictionary and in less than three minutes produce a list five pages long of reference material. While we were still making a futile attempt to shut our jaws and make our eyes retract back to their normal size, he apologized for having limited his search to university libraries located on the west coast of North America.

The sheer volume of information available through the Internet is both its greatest strength and weakness. No matter how obscure the destination you want to research, there will be information on it somewhere. As long as you have access to a power supply and a phone line, you can do follow-up or spur-of-the-moment research. For example, if a contact has been able to set up an unexpected backstage tour of London's Globe Theatre, you may want to brush up on your Shakespearean history before arriving. An hour or less on the Net should help you speak with "infinite variety" (*Anthony and Cleopatra*) about the man who helped make "all the world's a stage" (*As You Like It*) a "household word" (*King Henry V*).

The Internet is addictive to many people. If you're at all compulsive when researching, it's often easy to put off actually writing your article on Bora-Bora in favor of researching. Since no one can ever find out everything there is to know about a destination, you need to learn when to say "I have enough information. Now I will sit down and write."

Until you become experienced with how to narrow your search, many people find they are overwhelmed by the volume of information

It's easy to lose track of the amount of time you spend browsing the Net. If your server provides unlimited access, it doesn't matter if dinner time has come and gone, the rest of the family has watched three movies, and even the dog is asleep in bed before you finally turn off your computer. If, however, your server follows the more common procedure of charging an hourly rate after a certain free period each month, you may find yourself facing a nasty surprise when the bill arrives.

available. Many times there is so much material available that it's hard to know what to keep and what to discard.

2. Generate story ideas

Once you're armed with facts and fancies about your destination, begin generating ideas for articles and looking for suitable markets. Chapter 9 discusses in detail how to research markets and target suitable publications. (Don't forget about those consumer magazines discussed in chapter 1 that you might not usually think about as being suitable publications — food or sports magazines, for example.) Chapter 10 discusses the book market. Researching potential markets ahead of time can help generate article ideas and keep you focused.

What kind of information can form the basis of travel tales? Absolutely anything that captivates your interest. Here's a list to jump-start you in your search for potential story ideas:

- The area's natural environment.

- The geology. (Just how was the Grand Canyon formed?)

- Weather patterns. It's true, this isn't just a conversation opener on tours. Readers are interested in climate, seasons, and temperature — especially ones that produce disasters like tornadoes and avalanches.

- Government structure. It seems everybody everywhere loves to gripe about government policies.

- Predominant religions and how they affect the area's history and the daily lives of the locals. For example, the Indian belief in the sanctity of the cow has an impact on visitors and natives alike, yet is almost incomprehensible to most North Americans.

- How do people earn their living? What kinds of jobs and industries are there?

- How much does it cost to live there? What does a house cost? How much does food and entertainment cost?

- What kind of food is native to the area and how is it prepared? Are there traditional meals associated with various celebrations and festivals?

- What kinds of transportation are common? Throughout most of China, for instance, bicycles are not simply the politically correct "green alternative" they are in North America, they are often the only alternative to walking.

3. Send pre-trip query letters

Pre-trip query letters follow the same basic format as after-the-fact queries (chapter 9 discusses query letters in more detail). Begin your letter with a punchy lead, explain briefly why you are the perfect person to write the article, and ask if the editor is interested.

Send your pre-trip query early — several months at least and six months, if possible, before your trip. It's wise to inquire in your letter whether there is a particular slant or attraction the editor is especially interested in. For example, you may have dismissed the "psychic vortexes" of Sedona, Arizona, as being so much new age mumbo-jumbo that no one could possibly be interested in them. The editor you query, however, may realize, whatever his or her personal belief, these vortexes are the basis for a newsworthy story and one the publication's readership would enjoy.

Be sure to detail your departure and return dates. It's the source of endless frustration on both sides if you return home to discover a go-ahead letter for an attraction you didn't make time to visit.

4. Contact tourist bureaus and local attractions

Experts are often willing to share information which will add a special dimension to your visit. The opportunities for learning are almost endless: local archives, museums, the weather bureau, colleges, organizations for indigenous peoples, forestry personnel, theater facilities, even religious institutions.

Go ahead, ask for an hour of the planetarium curator's time or for a backstage tour of "The Met." The worst that can happen is the person will be too busy or say no. But it's amazing how often people are only too willing to say yes. Rick once got a spur-of-the-moment tour of a nuclear submarine simply by asking for it.

5. Check your equipment

One step that's vital, yet easy to overlook, is ensuring all your equipment is in working order. This includes cameras, laptop computers if you travel with one, tape recorders, and even pens. You only have to experience once the sinking feeling of your pen gouging a hole in your notepad to remember that a good pen (or more appropriately, a handful of good pens) is still the most invaluable tool any writer can own.

And now, at last, you're ready for the next step — enjoying your trip!

b. You're on your way — making the most of your travels

Taped inside the front cover of Susan's travel journal is a note a close friend gave her as a joke years ago.

Remember the Mighty Phylum Porifera!

A Phylum Porifera is a sponge, one of those remarkable water creatures that spend their entire lives absorbing the waters around them. And one of the most important habits a travel writer needs to cultivate is the ability to be a sponge. Or as a 16th-century proverb suggests, "the conscientious traveler must have the eyes of a falcon, the ears of a donkey, the back of a camel, the mouth of a whale, and the legs of a stag."

Travel is more than just foreign scenery; places aren't made up of just roads or plants or even buildings and history. Travel is about unknown cultures and attitudes to life, people of every skin tone imaginable, wealth and poverty, architectural triumphs and disasters, geography, seasons, sounds, smells, wildlife, and yes, scenery too. A travel writer must constantly hone his or her ability to absorb the new, unusual, and unexpected.

1. Don't forget the seasoning salt

Quick. Think about the last vacation you took. What's the first thing you recall? A monument? Perhaps the beach at sunset? Or maybe a herd of kangaroos?

Whatever your strongest memory, for most people it was probably a visual one. Many of us, especially in North America, have come to rely on visual images almost to the exclusion of the other four senses. While visual descriptions are an essential part of any travel piece, so are the other four senses — hearing, taste, touch, and smell.

Try to imagine walking through an open air market without smelling the fish, or visiting Disneyland without hearing the sound of children laughing. Can breakfast in a Parisian café be complete without the rich, creamy taste of a freshly brewed latté or cappuccino? And as any shopping enthusiast knows, the elegant sleekness of finely spun Chinese silk is part of its mystique and fascination.

Smell too is part of any good travel writing. Smell is also the single most overlooked element in most descriptions, even though it is a powerful motivator among both men and women. Talk to anyone in the perfume industry if you don't believe this.

Worksheet #1 is an exercise Susan uses to help students start reawakening a connection with their five senses. Inevitably, at the conclusion someone comments about a forgotten detail, usually a fragrance, and begins madly writing down notes. One woman approached Susan after class with an elated smile and told her, "I've always wondered why the smell of cinnamon always makes me think of San Diego, and now I finally remember."

When you do this exercise, be sure to include the last step — the emotions you are experiencing. While this isn't one of the five senses, an emotional response can sometimes become the focal point of an article. For example, during a visit to Arizona, Susan recalls being overwhelmed by a sense of ancient magic. It flowed from deep under the desert sands, watching and protecting. She eventually used that emotional response for a spin-off article about the influence of magic among early Indian cultures.

2. Expect the unexpected and capitalize on it

Opportunities are everywhere, but they are often sneaky and like to disguise themselves as unexpected problems and carefully laid plans gone wrong. Another word for adventure is sometimes "trouble."

One of Susan's student writer/photographers (we'll call him Paul), on a trip to England, had mapped out an entire feature about the many picturesque, medieval bridges dotting the countryside throughout the United Kingdom. He snapped photos and scribbled notes for an entire week. Each day he became more and more enthusiastic about the way his envisioned article was progressing. A quick sale was within reach.

Then disaster struck. The last two bridges, the focal point of the entire article (or so Paul had planned), were ruins of neglect. Worse yet, they were covered with graffiti and strewn with garbage. He felt his idea crumble along with the ancient rocks.

After he told this story in class, Susan asked if it excited anyone. Not one hand was raised. Why not? Because, the entire class had become caught up in Paul's misery that two unusable examples destroyed the original idea about picturesque English bridges.

The idea everyone overlooked was that this was actually an opportunity to write not one but two articles. When Susan suggested the original article plus a second piece about the tragedy of how

If you're having trouble incorporating all five senses into a particular piece, get a box of five different colored highlighters. Use one for each sense and go through a printout marking each place you use sight, smell, taste, touch, and hearing. You should end up with a manuscript resembling a five-colored rainbow.

REAWAKENING YOUR FIVE SENSES

The best way to do this exercise is to have someone read it out loud to you so your mind is totally free to recall images and sensations. If you have no one to help you, make a tape recording and play it back as you write. Either way, make sure you allow plenty of time (a minute or more in some cases) between paragraphs.

As you listen to the words, allow yourself to re-experience the destination using all five of your senses. Write down these impressions as fast as you can, and pay no attention to grammar, punctuation, or spelling. The idea is similar to brainstorming. Capture as many impressions as possible, and record them in whatever format you like. Once they're on paper, you can go back and develop story ideas from there.

Note: Some people prefer to shut their eyes, listen to the entire exercise, and then write everything down. Susan has tried this both ways and generally prefers to have people write as she reads. She can also gauge better which sections should have longer breaks between them because she can see when most people slow down.

Exercise:

Think about a favorite place you visited and return there in your mind.

Where are you? What are your surroundings like? Are you in a building, perhaps a restaurant, store, library, museum, market? Or are you outside, in a meadow, forest, watching giant surf pound the beach, looking down a snow-covered mountain or glacier?

What shapes and colors do you see? Are they angular steel and concrete or gently rounded straw thatch, red and gold embroidered cotton or gray clay pots, shiny or dull, monochrome or rainbow?

Look around at the other people. Who can you see? Laborers, gaudy tourists, young children playing, old people practicing Tai Chi on a lawn, a gang of punkers swinging chains, a rubby passed out in an alleyway?

Pick one person and watch him or her for several moments. How is this person dressed? What color skin does he or she have? Does this person seem happy or sad, old or young, carefree or worn with worry? Is he or she at work or at play? Does he or she make odd or expansive gestures or are the movements tight and reserved?

Now listen. What can you hear around you? The fizzing of a cappuccino machine, cars honking in a traffic jam, birds chirping, a tour guide speaking, children singing, music playing, a brook babbling?

What are the people here talking about? Are they speaking in English or another language? Are they laughing or serious? Do they sound happy or concerned? Are they whispering or shouting?

Inhale deeply and experience the aromas that are all around you. Are they pleasing — roses blooming, freshly baked bread, ocean breezes, a barn filled with warm hay? Or are they harsh and unpleasant — sweat, fish, cigarette smoke and stale booze, rotting vegetation?

What tastes can you experience here? The sweetness of cotton candy, the salt of beef jerky, the bitterness of burnt coffee, the exotic flavor of unknown spices, the tartness of a lemon rind?

Now extend your sense of touch to the things around you. What textures can you feel around you? The sleekness of a dolphin's back, the coarse wool of an Aran sweater, the velvet of an orchid petal, the warm smoothness of an ancient church pew?

What time of day is it? Is it winter or summer where you are? What is the weather like? Is the air clean and easy to breath or stuffy and polluted? What can you see down the street or out the windows?

Now turn your senses inward. What are you doing? Hiking along a mountain trail or sitting in a meditation garden, riding a bicycle or drinking lemonade, climbing a ladder or walking through a museum, taking photographs or enjoying the sun's warmth on your back? Feel the physical sensations in your body.

Finally, become aware of your emotions. Do you like the people and the scene around you? Would you like to stay here? Are you fatigued and bored or cheerful and excited? What would you like to say to the person you were watching? What do you think he or she would like to say to you? Where will you go next?

some of these ancient works of art are being defaced, murmurs of "Oh yeah" and "Never thought of that" ran through the classroom. Shared misery gave way to renewed interest.

Fortunately, Paul had four frames on his roll of film left when he reached the last two bridges. More out of desperation to use up his film than thinking of any kind of artistic merit, he'd shot some photos anyway. Using these photos he was able to work up a second article. True, the second piece required a different market, but Paul researched and found four potential homes for the new, darker piece. While we never heard whether or not he sold it, from our sneak preview, our money would be on a sale.

3. What on earth is that?

Sometimes a story opportunity is as simple as seeing something out of the ordinary and asking. Several years ago on an assignment trip to Ashland, Oregon, Susan noticed a small structure half way between her hotel and the downtown area. It was so untypically modern in its lines that she asked the hotel shuttle driver what it was. The driver's eyes shone with pride as she launched into a detailed accounting of the Pacific Northwest Museum of Natural History. The following morning, Susan squeezed an extra hour out of a jam-packed schedule, spoke with the PR department, and ended up with an entirely unexpected article about a unusual museum.

4. Hey, you mean there are people here too?

Many beginning travel writers are surprised to discover people are just as important to a well-written travel story as the destination is. But it is a rare destination indeed that has no people, and as Veronica Stoddart of Caribbean Travel and Life pointed out, "without people, a travel story is flat."

Experienced travel writers seek out contact with locals. We've sometimes learned more about an area talking to our unknown neighbor in an ice cream parlor than we did from reading dozens of brochures. With very little encouragement, the laughter strangers share — as their double chocolate fudge cones ripple over hands and drip elegantly onto laps — may develop into a treasure trove of personal anecdotes and truly "local" history. These are the gems that make a travel story live.

5. Look out — it's the information hound again!

No doubt about it, being a travel writer is going to turn you into an information scrounge. Pamphlets, newspapers, handwritten notes, postcards, local guide books all become fair game. When we're traveling, we try to gather everything in sight, ship it home, and worry about sorting through it later in the comfort of our favorite overstuffed armchair. Not only does it help refresh our memory, but we've often found nuggets of information we had missed on the trip itself.

For example, during an Alaska cruise through the Inside Passage, we faithfully collected copies of *Dagelyks Nieuws*, the ship's daily newsletter. Later we discovered they contained a wealth of little-known historical tidbits about the 49th state.

Here are some sources we've found helpful:

- Brochures from hotels and local attractions
- Chamber of Commerce and tourist bureau publications
- The local daily (or weekly) newspaper
- Freebie newspapers and magazines
- "The ten best things to see in . . . " guide books
- Map books (no kidding! Some of these have excellent notes)
- Menus
- Promotional flyers about everything from the newest musical in town to a newly opened condominium complex
- Postcards and other "tourist trap paraphernalia"

6. Have journal, will travel

> *I never travel without my diaries. One should always have something sensational to read in the train.*
>
> Oscar Wilde, *The Importance of Being Earnest*

When a traveler ventures into a new land, there is something unique about that first visit. The air smells different, the people may be a different color, the food has subtle (or not so subtle) differences in flavor and presentation. Perhaps you cannot even understand the language.

The ability to share these impressions is what separates a travel article that is nothing more than a recitation of facts and figures from one that sings with vibrancy and realism. Readers share the wonder, the contrast to what's known and expected, the *newness*.

Journals come in every imaginable size, color, style, and price. Some are $1, pocket-sized notepads; some are full-sized student exercise books; some are the hardcover notebooks that sell for $2 to $4 and are often available in knick-knack stores. Others sport hardcovers with pictures or other decorations.

Unfortunately, these first impressions that are so important to a travel article are the very ones that fade first and most completely.

No matter how many times we ask the question, "How many of you keep a journal when you're traveling?," we're still amazed by the number of student travel writers who don't. "What me? Keep a diary? You've got to be joking!" Many of these people have gone on truly incredible voyages — the Amazon, Patagonia, China, Russia, to name just a few. And yet the idea of recording their first impressions often hasn't occurred to them.

Most travel writers choose a journal for its practicality. Spiral-backed notebooks are popular because they are easy to fold back so you can write on both sides of each page.

However you make your own choice, here are some things to help you get the most out of this important travel writing tool.

(a) Record everything in as much detail as you can. Jot down notes, sketches, snippets of conversation — anything that captures your imagination or the atmosphere of the place you're visiting. What color hair did the waiter have who serenaded you at dinner? What did the parrot's claws feel like as he clung to your shoulder and pecked delicately at your ear? Did the priest who was napping at the gate to the temple snore? Remember — if it interested you, it will probably interest others too.

Format isn't important here, content is. We've seen some journals that are barely decipherable. Others look like a polished first draft of a finished article.

(b) Journals are usually written in while you're on the go. Look for a book in which you can write fairly comfortably while standing up. If it's still comfortable while you're not only standing up but jammed in the middle of a milling crowd, so much the better!

(c) Although you may seldom have this luxury, when you're actually able to spend some quiet time alone with your journal, you may want to color code your entries. This makes it easier for you to find relevant bits of information later. For example, you may want to use five different colored pens:

　(i) Black: general notes

　(ii) Red: important or unusual information that you want to find again easily

(iii) Blue: overheard conversations (these can add vibrancy and depth to a piece on local peoples)

(iv) Green: the landscape and scenery

(v) Purple: flights of fancy and daydreams inspired by being in a foreign land (What would it feel like to live in Buckingham Palace? Who are the spirits inhabiting the desert ruins of Tumacacori?)

    While this system is too cumbersome under most traveling situations, use it as an add on whenever you can.

(d) Never feel you have to show your journal to anyone else. If you choose to, that's fine. But knowing that whatever you write is completely private unless you decide otherwise will help you be honest in your notes.

(e) Treat your journal as a cherished traveling companion. Most professional travel writers would forget to pack their underwear before they forget to pack their journal.

7. The myth of the photographic memory

Many years ago, a TV program aired in which a man watched a string of numbered box cars lumber slowly past him down the railway track. There must have been over 50 cars, each with an identifying number of some dozen or more digits. When he sat down to recite the numbers from memory, he was perfect every time. But to this day, we wonder if he would have been able to describe what they *looked* like, or how the ground trembled, or even the sounds as they trundled past.

Mental images and impressions are fickle and ephemeral. Even though, at the time, it seems impossible that you'll ever forget the magnificence of the Taj Mahal or the grandeur of the Norwegian fjords, both memories fade as time passes.

The most important steps you can take on any trip are those which help you recall the journey so you can write about it. If you discover something helps you hang on to your impressions, use it as a tool, no matter how weird it may seem to others.

And now get set for the final job.

c. You're home — tidying up the loose ends

Once you're back from your travels, the real work of writing begins. But there are other things you should be doing in addition to writing.

1. Send thank-you notes

Courtesy is always correct. Unfortunately, it's also often overlooked or forgotten entirely. Make sure you are one of the people who remembers. Anyone who was of particular assistance should receive a short thank-you note within a week of your return.

2. Organize your notes and memorabilia

All the treasures you've picked up should be organized and either tossed out or filed for future use. Of course, it's impossible to keep everything; storage space for most of us is at a premium. It's one of those annoying ironies: no matter how long you've kept a piece of information, you'll need it within the first week after you finally decided to throw it out. One travel writer we know kept a city map of Bombay for seven years before she consigned it to the great round file. Two days later, she wanted a description of where two street intersected in — you guessed it — Bombay.

No one can tell you what to keep and what to pitch, but after a while you'll develop a "gut feeling" about certain things. As a rule of thumb, we try to keep anything that truly fascinates us (even if we can't see any possible way we'd use it in an article) or would be overly difficult to replace. In chapter 16, we'll help you design a way to organize your treasures.

3. Get your film developed

It sounds obvious, but you should get your film developed as soon as possible once you return home. Once you have the prints, label them! Your photographs will be unusable if you don't do this chore right away: will you remember whether it was a bomber or a transport plane four weeks later?

4. Send more query letters

Once you're safely home again, you'll most likely discover there are markets you hadn't thought of before. Perhaps you didn't realize before you left on your trip that Hong Kong had trails specially designed for city hiking or that an evening at a marvelous B&B with

While you're organizing all the material you've picked up en route, keep a pad of paper close by to jot down any new ideas for articles. Later you can brainstorm around any that look particularly promising.

Keep a photo log showing every shot you take while you're traveling. It may be a nuisance at the time, but you won't end up with a great photo you can't use because you don't remember what it is.

outdoor Jacuzzi overlooking the ocean the would be the result of a missed highway interchange. Check for possible markets and fire off as many proposals as possible.

5. Follow up on outstanding pretrip queries

If you still haven't heard back from any of the markets you queried before you left, now is a good time to send a "Hi, I'm back with a lot of great stories" letter. Keep it brief, the same as your original letter, but include a couple of specific teasers — the hiking trails in Hong Kong for example.

6. And finally — write!

Your stories are the grand finale. Work hard, but enjoy the writing as much as the trip.

7

Free trips

It's tough, but someone has to earn a living by sitting on a beach. As a travel writer, the job could be yours. But such trips don't come without effort. This chapter will guide you through the maze of asking for free trips. Or, to put it more delicately, help you find a sponsor for your trip. Asking the right way will get you more trips than most people could conceivably want.

When launching a marketing idea, the travel supplier must consider whether the return publicity will be worth the outlay. Although it is sometimes expensive — sending out press releases, running press trips, or sponsoring writers to visit their locale — most companies see publicity as a valuable return on their investment. State, provincial, and federal governments; tourist boards; airlines; hotels; resorts; dude ranches; cruise lines; and other travel suppliers all know a published recommendation by a travel writer has the same credibility as a word of mouth opinion from a friend — it's just heard by many more people.

Each year these organizations review how much effort and money they want to put into obtaining publicity. A lot of factors go into the decision. For example, a cruise line may be operating almost at capacity and feel it won't be able to accommodate any potential customers the publicity generates. Or a tourist board may have run a publicity campaign in the past year and feel everyone is tired of hearing about it. However, an organization may refuse a request this year and welcome it the next, as its budget and objectives change.

a. What to say

Before you call or write your selected sponsor, think about your project. It probably goes without saying, but some story hooks are better than others. Don't expect a glowing reception if you're planning an exposé on shark feeding habits at an island's beaches.

Prepare to convey your story angle in one or two sentences. Anything longer tells the sponsor that either your article is unfocused or you are working on a book, not an article.

Use a title even if it is not the one you think you will end up using. Something like, "this article is tentatively entitled 'Bed and Breakfasts in Hawaii,'" conveys the subject and tells the sponsor what angle you are pursuing.

If you are stuck for an idea, try a variation on these standbys: "The Inside Scoop on why XYZ is one of the best vacation values" or, "You don't have to spend a fortune to visit the secluded beaches of ABC." Your working title should be shamelessly promotional.

b. To call or to write?

There are two ways to solicit a trip. If you feel nervous about asking over the phone for what you want, simply ask for the name and title of the person who is responsible for sponsoring writers. Pitching your spiel on the phone is an acquired skill, so if this is your first request for a research trip, stick to writing letters. Letters give you time to consider and formulate what you want to say. Once you have a bit of experience and feel more confident, you can make your proposal over the phone.

We prefer to call and speak directly to the person in charge. Letters or faxes are cheaper, but they can be, and often are, ignored. Person-to-person contact gives you a quick grasp of what the supplier is looking for and a better feel for how enthusiastic (or unenthusiastic) he or she is.

Even if you don't have quite enough experience to feel confident doing your whole pitch over the phone, you can still obtain some valuable information with a couple of quick questions. Ask if the company ever sponsors writers on trips. If the answer is no, you don't need to waste time on correspondence.

If the company shows interest, however, find out if it would consider a proposal about your topic. Avoid a long discussion; you just want to know if it is worth your time to send material. If you can find the answers to these two questions in your first telephone conversation, you will vastly improve your efficiency. Also ask for suggestions or comments on what that sponsor would like to see in your story. For example you might ask, "Are there any specific points of interest you feel readers should know about your resort?"

Whichever way you solicit a trip, you will definitely spend some money on long-distance phone calls making arrangements. Although the cost of the phone calls will be a tiny percentage of the cost of a trip, it still adds up. A good phone plan will save you money. Call after prime-time hours. Calling before 8 a.m. if you are on the west coast or after 6 p.m. on the east coast still leaves you plenty of time to conduct business.

c. The proposal

Almost invariably you will need to write a proposal, even if you have spoken with someone on the phone and he or she is interested in your project. The proposal should contain a cover letter, your bio, and any letter of assignment you may have.

1. The cover letter

The cover letter should state a little about who you are and what the project is, as well as indicate how it will specifically benefit the sponsor. Tell your potential sponsor exactly what you require — the more specific the better.

If you can obtain a firm commitment for publication, mention it in your cover letter and include a copy of the letter of assignment. You should state the publication, the issue the article will appear in, and your deadline.

2. Your bio

Your proposal to a potential sponsor should include a cover letter, bio, and an assignment letter if you have one. Don't forget your business card.

You should tailor every bio you send to the sponsor. You may want to emphasize particular articles that most closely resemble the sort of write-up you will do on that sponsor. Chapter 13 discusses in more detail how to write a bio.

Don't send copies of articles. Mention that copies of previous articles are available on request as one of the last sentences of your proposal. It will keep your costs down. Oddly enough, we are rarely asked for them. Sample #4 gives an example of a letter to send a sponsor regarding a research trip.

January 12, 199-

Joe White
One of the Islands
Whitsunday, Australia

Dear Mr. White:

I will be doing a 1,500 word feature article for *Let's Travel* magazine about cruising the islands of the Whitsunday. The article, presently entitled "Sailing the 'Sundays," will include sidebar material with recommendations for transportation, accommodation, and things to see. My recommendations will appeal to the middle-income and upscale readers; this is not a backpacker story. Photos will be included, so I would appreciate any professionally done pictures you may be able to give me.

Let's Travel is a national, subscription-only travel magazine. Readers are fairly evenly distributed across Canada and the United States and have middle to high incomes. They are primarily interested in getting value for their travel dollar, hearing about interesting places, and learning how to stay safe while traveling.

As you can see from my publications list, I am adept at media exposure for my sponsors. My strategy is to make the time and effort put into research on any topic stretch to as many articles and interviews as possible. I believe the topic I have chosen is perfect for a long-term campaign.

What I request is accommodation at your hotel for a portion of the time I am there. I expect to be in your area April 6 to April 10, 199-.

Thank you very much for your time.

Sincerely,

Terri C. Brown
Enclosure

d. Who ya gonna call? — Finding the right contact

Most potential sponsors want to hear from you. They have a mandate to entice people to visit their destination, fly their airline, cruise on their ships. No one turns down publicity without thinking it through.

Every organization has different commitments to obtaining publicity. You may deal with someone who has many other jobs, and speaking with writers is a tiny and marginal part of his or her responsibilities. When the commitment is larger, the organization may do public relations in-house through its public relations department or have a person in the marketing department who spends most of his or her day working with the media. Alternatively, that person may refer you to an outside public relations company which handles any media inquiries.

Ask for the public relations (PR) department of a potential sponsor as a first step to any new project. Public relations responsibilities are sometimes handled by corporate communications or the media department. They will be able to direct you to the person to address your proposal to.

If you are transferred to the advertising or sales department, politely ask if someone there handles publicity. We never deal with the sales or advertising departments. Sales departments manage affairs with travel agents; advertising departments field calls from newspapers and magazines that are trying to convince the sponsor to spend money with them.

If you make the mistake of trying your pitch on someone from either department, you'll receive a very cool reception. The phrases, "We have already used up our advertising budget for the year" or, "What agency did you say you were with?" are clues that you were misdirected.

e. The players

1. In-house public relations

Especially with small travel suppliers, the person who makes the decisions about how much publicity you might bring them is also often in charge of several other things. You might find, for instance, that the president of the company will hear your proposal directly. In other cases, the company may come to a decision based on your proposal and then give the necessary authorization to one of its secretaries to implement. Either way, you get quick decisions and implementation.

It can be dicier when a low level staffer with no training and no back-up is given the PR job. He or she doesn't have the authority to make decisions and may not be able to persuade the decision-maker to read what is sent. This can be very frustrating for everyone involved. Unless this supplier is the only one who goes to your chosen destination, it's easier to simply move on to another supplier.

2. Public relations firms

Some organizations prefer to farm out this kind of work to public relations firms. All requests for information, pictures, and free trips go through the PR firm that sifts out the best possibilities and presents them to its client along with a recommendation.

Public relations companies are usually a joy to work with. They are used to handling the media and can almost anticipate your needs. It is also easy to please them. They live and die by the number and quality of media reports about their client that can be shown to be a direct result of work they do. All you have to do is send a steady stream of articles about their clients to make a friend for life (or until the client changes PR firms, whichever comes first).

3. Tourist boards

Tourist boards normally do their own public relations — but not always. You can accurately think of them as public relations firms with just one client, usually a government.

If you are planning to write about a destination, the tourist board is a great place to start. In many cases, they can be the intermediary between you and airlines, hotels, resorts, tourist attractions, car rental companies, and every other conceivable type of travel supplier. As well, they will often take on the responsibility of arranging and coordinating your entire trip.

As an example, on a trip to Australia, one of the tourist boards put together a one-week itinerary that had Rick and Barbara visiting seven completely different hotels or resorts, numerous attractions, and had also arranged all the transportation in between. All they did was talk to the tourist board a few times and write the articles after they got back.

f. How hard can it be?

You know you have made it when you can have a trip anywhere your heart desires and someone else pays for it. The sponsor obviously thinks of you as a writer with an audience it wants to reach. But some suppliers are targeted so much by writers and would-be writers that they are leery about giving anything away free. Here's how to court even the most reticent among them.

1. Airlines

Airlines are the hardest supplier to pry a free trip from. Because there are a only a few dozen of them shared among thousands of travel writers looking for freebies, most airlines painstakingly screen writers. Many of the airlines have officially stopped giving any kind of freebies except those for writers from the most prestigious publications.

You will have the best luck with small regional and overseas airlines. Small regional airlines do not receive many requests from writers because their destinations are usually limited to less tourist-oriented places. If you have a project where you can use these small airlines, it should be easy.

Overseas airlines, especially flag carriers (national, or government-owned carriers), want more business to come to their home base. From their point of view, they want writers to reach readers in their overseas market. They have an incentive to help you.

Airlines have also caught on to the fact that it is hard to write about them. Unless you are doing a piece specifically about the airline, it is difficult to discuss the airline within an article without sounding a bit off your main topic.

Most writers do include the airline name in the sidebar material, and for some companies this is sufficient. Some airlines, however, have concluded a free ticket traded for one mention in a sidebar is not a very good exchange and now give away free tickets only to writers doing pieces on the airline itself. Others still feel that if you are writing about their destination, it will generate business for them.

The overriding consideration for all airlines is how full their loads are to a particular destination. This year an airline may have plenty of paying passengers on their European routes but need a little help on their routes to Asia. Go with the flow. Find a story to write on

Asia. Or wait till next year. Things may have changed and they may need to boost Europe again.

The Internet gives you access to a comprehensive list of destinations to which the different airlines fly. Or, you can call around to the airlines directly. We discourage you from using travel agents. They are commissioned salespeople; using them for freebie information is a waste of time for them and, ultimately, for you.

Seasonality may have a huge influence on airlines' response. Don't bother requesting a free seat to anywhere during peak Thanksgiving or Christmas seasons. Airlines will very often offer you standby space only. If you don't need to meet a deadline, and you don't need to travel long distances to the airport — where you may discover that you are not going to get on the flight — it may be worthwhile. But, if you are meeting a ship or have some other immovable deadline, do not accept standby. Ask for confirmed positive space. We always specify deadlines in our proposals to let them know why we need confirmed seats.

2. Cruise lines

The cruise industry is expanding at an incredible rate. Huge new vessels are coming on stream with hundreds of cabins to be filled. There are still a huge marketplace of people who have never cruised, and their business is much sought after.

Many cruise lines are hungry for articles about these people. You should be able to procure a free cruise if your project can promise some publicity for the line.

Some cruise lines, on the other hand, are doing so well they will not give you a free cabin. Instead they may charge you a preferred rate of 75% off the brochure rate. Unless you have a particular reason for sticking with that particular line, for example, a specialized story line, move on to the next one.

Unlike airlines, information on cruise ships is easy to get. Go to your local travel agency and pick up a brochure on ships sailing to the destinations you are researching.

Although we've used the expression "free," very little is completely so. When a cruise line agrees to give you a cabin, there are still several money-sapping things to consider before you agree to do the trip. Most cruise lines do not pay for port taxes or charges, which can range up to $200 for a week-long cruise. Typically the cruise line will not pay for your airfare to get to the cruise ship either, although there are exceptions.

If you have ever been on a cruise ship, you know shore excursions in each port can be a big part of the experience. Some writers' trips include a few free excursions, but generally you'll be expected to pay for any extra sights you want to see. Even if you don't take pre-arranged shore excursions, you can expect to incur some costs while seeing the port. We find that once we've traveled all that way, we can justify spending a few dollars more to see a sight which we may not see ever again. Be sure to ask if any excursions are included at no charge with your cruise.

Tips are another hidden expense of your freebie and can cost up to $200. Some cruise lines will offer to pay for your tips to cabin stewards; some sail to destinations that do not allow tipping. Tahiti's culture, for instance, does not encourage tipping, and the custom of not tipping is followed on board, too.

Some writers reason that because they are working, they should not tip. Be sure you ask about the ship's tipping policy so you know what to expect.

All in all, a "free" cruise can easily cost you $2,000 for two people if you do not pay attention to the extras. Be sure to discuss each of these with your contact at the cruise line. Some of these extras may be negotiable.

3. Hotels and resorts

The problem you may encounter with hotels is similar to that of airlines. You can write only so much about a hotel before it begins to sound like an advertisement. The good news is that there are thousands of hotels and most are happy to provide a room in exchange for a mention. Publicity opportunities do not come to the majority of hotels with any frequency, so they are usually delighted.

As you would expect, hotels in out-of-the-way places are more excited at the prospect of your visit than those in palm tree-infested islands. Still, even in Hawaii where every writer eventually asks for a free room, there are plenty of takers.

g. Press trips

Press trips, or FAM (familiarization), trips can be fun if you like traveling with a group of other writers; writers are invited to a resort or area for a comprehensive tour. You can obtain a detailed itinerary before you say yes to make sure it is really something you are interested in.

The advantage of a press trip is that you don't usually have to have a specific article in mind before you go, so you can go just to gather information. Press trips are a terrific way to do research quickly. They are normally jammed with places to see and things to do.

Usually everything is paid for, including many meals, entrance fees to attractions, priority entry to attractions (no waiting in line-ups — a must at tourist-clogged places like Universal Studios or Disneyland where line ups can be lengthy), ground and sometimes air transportation, and special lectures or demonstrations.

Press trips also allow you to have meals with other writers and network as you travel.

The major complaints about FAM trips, we hear, are these:

(a) There is not enough free time to explore your own interests.

(b) Some are so full, they amount to an endurance test and you should count on a few days off to recuperate once you get home. A very wearing itinerary might have you meeting tourist board representatives for a breakfast briefing right after an all-night flight, or it might have you dropping in to tour a dozen different hotels before noon each day for the official spiel. London for the weekend from the west coast is only fun once.

When we are interested in a high-speed, high-energy trip, we pick press trips that are going to cover a lot of ground — everything you wanted to know about Malaysia in one week, for instance.

h. The independent itinerary

We can only stand the hurried pace of most press trips about once a year. Most of the time we put together our own itinerary which gives us more time to explore.

Developing your own research trip is a lot more work. You need to set up a day-by-day plan of where you want to go and then contact individual hotels and attractions in the area about complimentary lodging or admission.

We try to use tourist boards in the area. Many times they are glad to approach hotels on your behalf and make suggestions as to what you should see. Many trips are a mix. Tourist boards will sometimes have you changing hotels every night so you can experience a range of accommodation. We generally find some places on our own, in addition to the tourist boards' arrangements; it allows us to control the pace of the trip better.

The big advantage of working with tourist boards is that they usually aim to please and already know of some of the premiere places and things to do. More over, they know the little details about their area that can make or break a research trip. For example, it might look like a short distance to a Greek ruin but, in fact, what you can't see is that the roads are virtually inaccessible and require an all-terrain vehicle.

When you embark on designing an independent itinerary, whether it is with hotels or tourist boards, the secret is to be straight-forward and concise about what you are looking for.

i. Family and friends

There are no rules about companions going with you for free. Many suppliers realize you are working and away from home and after the first hundred trips, it may be hard to entice you to travel by yourself.

Cruise lines and hotels usually willingly invite a companion. After all, the room or cabin has already been reserved for you and they can look like good guys without much more of an expense by including someone you want to travel with. When free space cannot be offered, they will often suggest a deeply discounted rate. If they don't, it doesn't hurt to ask if they have "preferred rates for companions."

Airlines have mixed policies. If you can show that your companion is also a writer or photographer with different outlets than yourself, you shouldn't have much problem.

j. Ethics and the bad trip

Barbara once went on a deluxe cruise where diners had to line up the first night for up to three hours before being seated, honeymoon-ers were assigned bunk beds, exhaust from the ship's stack flooded the ventilating system and covered everything from tooth brushes to tuxedos in a miasma of black smeary soot, and several strangers were given the same cabin. She never did hear whether they com-plained.

So did she write a scathing report about her host? Nope. Most of the problems were due to a computer foul-up which was unlikely to be repeated. And the ship was days away from going in for a major refit. Presumably the ventilator problem would be corrected before the ship's return to the high seas.

After refit, the ship would be returning to do the same wonderful itinerary, and the ports of call would remain as spectacular as ever. The only thing she felt consumers needed to be gently warned about was the service of some of the crew. With the extra pressure of all the bad luck, she gave them the benefit of the doubt: the poor service was mentioned but not stressed.

To be sure, we have all written articles that absolutely warned customers away from destinations for health or safety reasons and we have complained in print about service. However, these were the result of ongoing attitudes, not one-time problems.

Are we influenced by the bottle of champagne and fruit basket in the room when we arrive? Yep. We feel very grateful. We will be sure to send a personal thank-you note for the thoughtfulness. And we will still write that readers shouldn't go out in this part of town without a hotel employee with them or that the rooms were mouldy or musty.

Sometimes we write nothing at all. When we can't figure out if what happened to us would happen to any other traveler, we figure we can't contribute a useful opinion. Bad service by one employee does not mean all the staff are terrible. We might personally have a rotten experience and still write a good review. It is also useful to hear how fellow travelers are reacting to the same experiences.

There is a myth that travel writers are singled out for special treatment and can never really know what the average person will experience. Rubbish. Writers eat the same food, walk on the same beach, and sleep in the same accommodation as everyone else. If the myth were true, we would have never come across bad service, and we certainly cannot make that claim.

The only way a sponsor has tried to influence what we think of its airline or destination was by being very helpful and making sure we had a smooth trip. We have never had a sponsor even suggest what it would like to see in an article. Occasionally, we ask if there is something about a place which is particularly colorful or an angle it is currently pushing that we might not have thought of. We listen and sometimes use the suggestions we get.

Every writer's philosophy about when and how hard to bite a travel supplier's hand is different. Here are some things to keep in mind:

(a) Boring destinations are not automatically cause for a negative report. Rick hated the shopping mecca of St. Thomas in the Virgin Islands, but most of his ship-board companions loved the whole experience. So he let the reader know exactly what the experience was about.

Those who love to shop will find a trip there an exhilarating experience. Without ever saying anything negative, everyone else will be warned off. The travel suppliers will acquire passengers who love what they have to offer. The passengers will tell everyone they know about the fabulous deal they got. In short, everyone will be happy.

(b) Lousy weather and fluctuating currencies are forces of nature, yet we have seen writers complain in print about the lousy time they had because of the weather. By all means, warn your readers about the rain in England, but don't condemn the entire place for it.

(c) Unappetizing food or decrepit accommodation is something most travel suppliers do have some control over. But then, some people eat spaghetti every night and any change in the menu is heaven. Others go on holidays to spend their entire time on the beach and couldn't care less about the state of the room, as long as it is cheap and bug-free. The fact is, most travel suppliers stay in business because they offer a product which somebody, somewhere, thinks is terrific. Be aware that your negative opinion isn't necessarily shared by everyone.

(d) We try to give the supplier some leeway when there is trouble and focus on the good points of a trip, but we are unequivocal when it comes to safety and health concerns. If a gang of thugs targets tourists at a destination, our readers will hear about it.

Sometimes reports are conflicting, especially in countries with an exciting political life. We prefer to tell the reader both the official version and what we are getting from other sources. Let the traveler decide how much risk he or she wants to take. Some travelers hate a holiday without some excitement to it.

(e) The most important point is still to remember your audience when you choose your sponsor. If you are writing an article for a publication aimed at travelers wanting first class, stick with first-class products. Don't seek out budget hotels and then have nothing nice to say.

k. Timing

Plan to do your research at your destination in the off season. The public relations people will have more time for you, there are usually a lot of hotel rooms or ship's cabins standing empty, and there are fewer crowds. Don't even think of asking for a free hotel in Hawaii at Christmas or in New Orleans at Mardi Gras. If your story is about Mardi Gras, start asking well in advance, be prepared to pay for it yourself, and come up with an amazing story hook.

Start working on your request for sponsorship as soon as you can. Six months before your travel date is good if the itinerary is complicated. Three months is usually adequate, unless you are dealing with a country which has a reputation for slowness. Italy, Mexico, and India come to mind.

Politics can also affect your plans. One writer told us that every time she talked to the tourist board about her trip, the public relations person had changed because a new government was in power.

It *is* possible to put together a trip in much less time than six months. If the itinerary is simple, you can do it quickly. Our record is four days.

Keep in mind that no matter how far in advance you make your pitch, many times your request might be processed, but your trip will not be finalized until perhaps a month prior to departure. We've run into this several times with cruise lines. The sponsor wants to make sure the space won't be sold before giving it away.

l. Paperwork

Always have all commitments in writing and carry the letters with you on your trip. It pays to have your paperwork very organized. On almost every trip we have taken, there's been something that has not gone as expected. A signed letter gives the person in front of you immediate authorization to solve the problem, even if he or she is unable to contact head office.

Once when Barbara had a 5 a.m. flight, she arrived at the airport only to find there was no reservation for her. The people at the front counter looked at her authorization letter and got her on the flight. Without the letter, she would have wasted a full day while the reservation staff waited for head office to open to fax them the appropriate documentation. She would have missed her sailing

---

Eight steps to a free trip

1. Have a solid story angle in mind ahead of time.

2. Avoid requesting space during major holidays or sporting events unless it is imperative to your story.

3. Make a list of potential sponsors. Find out which carriers, cruise lines, hotels and resorts service the area you want to go to.

4. Call or fax to find out the name of the contact person in public relations. If you get the name of the head of advertising, ask again for the public relations person, and stress you are a writer.

5. Call the potential sponsor, or write a query letter highlighting the idea of your story. Ask for suggestions on what that sponsor would like to see in your story.

6. Send the sponsor your proposal and follow up with a phone call a couple of days later. Continue to follow up at one-week intervals if you are not getting a response.

7. To be on the safe side, have alternative plans in mind. When dealing with sponsors, it's not unusual to leave on a trip with at least one segment or a hotel room not yet completely confirmed.

8. Follow up by sending out thank-you notes and copies of any clippings.

date. No reservation personnel will ever let you onto an airplane or into a hotel room on just your say so.

We have been able to resolve every conflict that has arisen because we had the correct documentation to back up our claims. More than once we have had a commitment from a tourist board or travel supplier to sponsor us and then watched with some apprehension as staff lost the paperwork, went on vacation, or changed jobs without briefing our new contact. But it has always worked out. To reassure you, once you have a commitment, you can usually relax and let the supplier fret about how to issue documents and deliver them to you.

m. Keep in touch

Be sure to write thank-you notes. Developing a relationship with someone in the company is your ticket to more invitations to other places the company goes to or represents. It will also mean a quick response to your queries for information when you next need background information for an article.

No matter who you deal with, always be sure your contact gets a copy or fax of anything you write once it is published. When it is a radio or TV interview, we normally call and let that contact know about it. Occasionally, we're asked for a tape, and if we anticipate the request, we'll try to arrange for a copy to be made.

n. To be free or not to be free

It is important to be aware there are publications that will not accept submissions from writers who have accepted any kind of freebie. They feel an evaluation is biased when a trip is free.

Some publications, however, will pay for writers on assignment. This is vital, as few writers would be able to afford the cost of trips without some sponsorship.

Do your homework on the publication you are targeting before you spend all your time getting a free trip, only to find it's useless for the publication you have lined up.

8
Putting your best manuscript forward

At last! An editor wants to see your manuscript. Like everything else, there's a right way and a wrong way to present your article. This is your last chance to demonstrate true professionalism, so get set to make your manuscript look as polished and professional as possible.

If you think a "unique-looking" manuscript is a good way to get the editor's attention, you're probably right. Unfortunately, it's usually the wrong kind of attention. One editor we know actually refused to take a manuscript from the post office because of its unique envelope — black with silver spider webs and wide-eyed bats. Who knows, perhaps it contained the greatest article ever written on spelunking in France. But this editor wasn't prepared to take the chance that it was something more than just another weirdo's cheap trick to gain her attention.

There are books devoted entirely to formatting every type of manuscript, from poems to trilogies. Here are the main points to be aware of when you send your manuscript off to a publisher. Some things will make sense; some may seem arbitrary. But you can be sure if you don't follow these basic rules of presentation, you'll automatically be labeled as, at best, an amateur and, at worst, a crackpot. Either way, you'll be taking several steps backward along the road to publication.

(a) *Paper.* Use plain, white paper; 20-pound bond is best. Erasable paper, onion skin, or pretty pastel colors look wonderful for letters to friends and family. They look amateurish for manuscripts.

(b) *Spacing.* It's tempting to demonstrate environmental awareness and concern by single spacing your work and printing on both sides of the page. This is fine for your working drafts, but when you send in a manuscript, grit your teeth and print single-sided, double-spaced copy with at least one-and-a-half inch margins all round (top, bottom, and sides).

This makes the document much easier to read and gives the editor somewhere to jot down notes to the typesetter and proofreader, if your manuscript is accepted for publication. Remember to indicate the beginning of a new paragraph by using the tab key to indent five spaces.

(c) *Font.* Use a clear, easy-to-read font such as Times New Roman, Garramond, or Courier, in 10 or 12 point. Cutesy or arty fonts such as Beehive, Cookie Hollow, or Trufflette belong on those pretty pastel letters to Grandmum.

Underline any words you want italicized, even though the italics button on your keyboard looks so simple and tempting. Underlining is the typesetter's code for italicizing.

(d) *Margins.* Never use full justify — the feature that makes the print flush on both right and left edges. Full justification creates variable spacing between the letters and increases the number of words per page. Experienced editors can look at a manuscript and estimate the word count as long as it isn't full justified.

(e) *Author information.* Print your real name (rather than your pen name), address, and phone number in the upper lefthand corner of the cover page (if you are writing a book) or first page (if you are writing an article). If you have a fax number, e-mail address, or agent, place this information directly below.

(f) *Word count.* The word count of your manuscript goes in the upper righthand corner of your cover page (books) or first page (articles). It should be approximate, which usually means rounded off to 100 or 1,000. (We round to the nearest 50 if the article is less than 1,000 words.)

Using your computer's word-count feature to give the exact word count flags you as an amateur to most editors, so resist the temptation to say you have "638 words," and settle for "approximately 650 words."

(g) *Rights*. Many writers indicate which rights are being offered directly below the word count. (See chapter 18 for more details on rights, copyright, and other legal issues). This used to be a standard, but is now considered optional or, in some cases, undesirable. Overall, we still recommend that you state, up front, which rights you are selling.

(h) *Manuscript title and author name.* Center and underline your title just above the middle of the page. Indicate the name you want printed with your work, two lines below the title. If you are writing a book, leave the rest of the page blank and start on the next sheet. If you are writing an article, drop four to six lines and begin your text.

Note: Pseudonyms or pen names are strictly a matter of preference. Okay, so it's ego, but personally, we can't imagine seeing anything other than our real names on any of our writing. There's nothing quite like the thrill of seeing your name in print. Be proud of it!

However, there are some very valid reasons why people elect to use one.

- A married woman may want to use her maiden name, especially if she's already built a reputation.

- If your name is difficult to spell or pronounce, it's sometimes better to write under a more easily remembered name.

- If your name has connotations you feel may turn readers away, you may want to consider using a pseudonym. Adelle Hitler, Frank D'Eath, or even Paul Jesus could all cause unnecessary friction or even unconscious rejection by some readers.

- If you have already built a reputation in a different genre, for example, if you have become well-known for your erotica short stories or western novels, using a different name for your travel tales could help avoid being typecast as a writer who specializes only in the one genre.

(i) *Running heads*. Print your name and the title of your article on the upper lefthand corner of every page except the cover/first page. Show page numbers on the upper righthand corner of all but the cover/first page. You never know when your pages may get scattered over the floor of an editor's office.

If you have a title of more than four or five words, use a "slug" or shortened version to identify which story the page is from (you should also consider shortening the title).

(j) *Last page.* At the bottom of your last page, type either -END- or -30- centered on the page. The -30- format comes from the days when typesetters actually laid out lead type in a tray, although we have never been able to discover why this particular number was chosen.

Sample #5 shows how your manuscript should look when you send it to an editor.

Editors hate staples. Use paper clips to hold your work together.

(k) *Printing.* A laser printer is nice, but it isn't an absolute necessity — yet. It probably will be soon. Although the occasional editor has stated right in his or her guidelines that dot-matrix printouts will be returned unread, most won't reject your manuscript based on the type of printer you use.

What can, and often does, cause a rejection is using a dot-matrix printer with a faded ribbon. Always invest in a ribbon that will print clear, dark type. It's a fact of life that when faced with a never-ending stack of manuscripts measured in feet rather than inches, many editors will put aside the ones they can't read clearly.

Although many publishers are now accepting work on disk, never assume this will be okay without specific instructions from the editor. It's courteous to offer, but wait until asked before sending, and always ensure you know what program and format (Mac or IBM compatible) the editor wants.

(l) *Corrections.* It used to be okay to have a few corrections on a manuscript if they were neatly done, the theory being they showed you were conscientious enough to check the manuscript over before sending it to the publisher. Because of the convenience of computer printouts, this is now a subject that's open to some debate. We prefer to have each page perfect. If we see an error, we reprint the entire page.

Remember, editors are notoriously overworked professionals, but they are only human. When faced with a choice between ten easy to read manuscripts in correct format and ten requiring "special handling" just to scan through, you can guess which ones they'll most likely read. Use Sample #5 as a template to ensure every manuscript you send out reflects your professionalism and dedication to your craft.

Sample #5
Manuscript submission format

Ambitious Author (your real name)   Approx. word count: 650
946 Writer's Blvd.   First serial rights
Vancouver, BC V7K 2K2
Tel: (604) 555-2233
Fax: (604) 555-2223
stami@web.ca
Donna McClean (agent's name if you have one)

How to submit a manuscript
by
Susanne Tami *(the name you want printed with your book or article)*

Start here if you are writing an article. Leave the rest of the page blank and start on the next

sheet if you are writing a book.

It used to be okay to have a few corrections on a manuscript as long as they were neatly

done, the theory being they showed you were conscientious enough to check it over before

sending it out. Because of the convenience of computer printouts, this is now a subject that's

open to some debate. My preference is to have each page perfect. If I see an error, I reprint the

entire page.

Remember, editors are notoriously overworked professionals, but they are only human.

When faced with a choice between ten easy-to-read manuscripts in correct format and ten

requiring "special handling" just to scan through, you can guess which ones they'll most likely

read. Use this sample as a template to ensure every manuscript you send out reflects your

professionalism and dedication to your craft.

- 30 -

9
Selling to newspapers and magazines

This chapter will help you get your first paying projects. There are no big secrets to be revealed or short cuts that will slice your time in unpublished purgatory in half. The fact is, if you think like a salesperson, pursue your dream in a businesslike fashion, and stick with it, you will end up as a published travel writer.

The easiest way to get started is to be a freelancer. Anyone can start immediately — no job application and no previous experience necessary. Freelance just means you don't work as an employee for anyone.

Barbara and Rick work as freelance columnists. In other words, they do not have any obligation to continue their columns nor do any of the publications they write for have any obligation to pay them unless those publications decide to publish their work.

Most travel writing jobs are like this. Some magazines and newspapers have travel editors, but they rarely have staff who do nothing but travel and write stories. It is far more common for staff who are already responsible for writing other sections of the newspaper or magazine to write about trips they take.

In addition to these employees, syndication companies supply some of the editorial for the travel section in most newspapers and a few magazines. These companies put together travel stories that appear in dozens or hundreds of newspapers across Canada and the United States.

The newspaper pays a pittance for these articles, sometimes as little as $5. The articles are well written, topical, and extremely easy to acquire, since articles are downloaded electronically at predetermined prices. Editors don't have any article-by-article negotiations to contend with, as they do when they deal with a freelancer. However, editors who want to see a particular destination emphasized or have an exclusive article for the newspaper usually need to look for another source. That's where freelancers come in.

Both magazines and newspapers use freelance articles to round out what they offer to the public. The catch is that what you offer must be fresh, exclusive, and inexpensive in order to compete with staffers and syndicates. The hard reality is you probably aren't going to get paid what your effort is worth if it's published only once. So to make this a worthwhile venture, you'll have to adopt some strategies to make the most of your research and writing.

a. Teaching a hard-working dog new tricks

To sell your travel articles, you must cultivate a set of skills and attitudes that have nothing to do with writing travel articles. Many people love to polish their prose almost indefinitely. They might write terrific pieces but refrain from any attempt to sell them because they think that would be too mundane and commercial.

Ideally, you want to have a specific audience in mind before you ever touch the keyboard or pick up your pen. As you become more experienced, your knowledge base of what different magazines and newspapers publish will increase, and you'll automatically frame themes and hooks to fit particular publications.

For example, as well as wanting to share the tranquillity of a sunset with the reader, you'll find yourself thinking, "XYZ magazine loves articles about Caribbean sunsets. I bet I can sell it a story about how different tourists greet the evening. And which other publication would be willing to buy it?"

The transformation from writer to writer/marketer is the turning point for all amateur writers. Every travel writer eventually realizes he or she does not want to work as hard as is necessary to create a perfect travel piece without getting paid for it. So here is how you start earning money.

b. Step one: know your market

1. Sample your potential market

Ideally, you should read cover to cover the five or six most recent issues of any magazine you want to submit to. Check your local library, and don't be afraid to ask if you don't see the magazine you're looking for. Libraries can often get publications from other branches even if they don't normally carry it themselves.

If you've tried the libraries, you've asked all your friends, and even your doctor's office doesn't carry it (no kidding: sometimes you can find the most amazing publications scattered over the coffee table in the waiting room), write the magazine for a sample issue.

Many magazines will publish the rate for a sample issue, as well as a subscription, on the masthead. If not, a fairly good rule of thumb is to take the single issue price and add 20% to cover the extra mailing cost and handling. Even if this isn't quite what a publication normally charges for a sample, there are very few that won't put one in the mail after you've shown good faith in sending a check.

There's an increasing trend among U.S. banks to insist that all checks be drawn on a U.S. bank. Canadian checks are sometimes refused, even if they are drawn on a U.S.-dollars account at a Canadian bank. (We have not heard of the reverse being a problem.) Even though a money order is more expensive, it may save you irritation and delay.

One word of caution about ordering a magazine from a different country: be aware of the differences in currency values, denominations, and symbols. Susan once sent a request to a U.K. publication and inadvertently put a dollar sign instead of a pound sterling sign in front of the Visa authorization. This meant a month's delay in getting the sample because the magazine had to write back to confirm she was really authorizing a £5 charge (at that time the equivalent of $12.50) to Visa, rather than a $5 charge.

If you are planning to target newspapers, you are probably better off reading several recent issues to check for tone, style, and focus than you are asking for back issues.

2. Analyze the publications

There is really only one rule of marketing: know thy market before submitting!

Perhaps because it sounds so straightforward, it's amazing how often this simple rule is overlooked. But as any experienced writer knows, the surest way to increase your supply of rejection slips is to submit an article or book proposal to an inappropriate publisher.

Granted, newspapers tend to have a broader audience, so it is harder to define their readership (and they don't usually send out rejection slips either — they simply don't publish the piece!), but you will still benefit from reading this discussion if you plan to target newspapers.

For example, *Trailer Life* is not going to be a likely prospect for an article, however well written, on an adventure tour to the Antarctic — a destination with marvelous penguins, but no roads and nothing even vaguely resembling trailer parks. *Trailer Life*'s readers have no reason to be interested. For people whose sole travel interest is trailering, this destination offers little. Nor would a science fiction magazine be likely to publish anything about the wonders of traveling by cruise ship, at least, not cruise ships on this world. As offbeat as these examples sound, such misdirected submissions are common. So how do you target likely magazines? Read the magazine before you submit. Reading several issues (or even one) is, without question, the best way to increase your chances with a particular magazine. Sound simple? It is.

But reading a magazine with an eye for potential markets is a very different proposition than reading one strictly for pleasure or even destination/travel information. You won't have the luxury of skipping over sections that seem uninteresting or not relevant to your own interests. You must read everything: masthead, bylines, sidebars, subscription information, even the advertisements. Every one of these components will give you valuable clues and insights into what the editors expect from the articles they choose to publish.

At this point in most travel writing classes, someone asks, "You don't really mean read all the advertising do you? Ads are only another way for the magazine to make money. Why should I waste my time reading *them*?"

Because ads are like signposts about the readership. Let's look at two hypothetical travel magazines and examine five ads out of each one.

Magazine #1:

- Mercedes Benz
- Russian vodka
- Investment opportunities abroad
- Rolex watches
- Holland America Cruise Line

Take a moment to think about the implication of these advertisements. Your aim is to establish as much information as possible about the *average* reader of Magazine #1. Some of the questions you should be asking include:

- What is the probable age range?
- What about income level?
- What kind of work do they do?
- What level of education have they reached?
- What's their main reason for reading this particular publication?

Here is a typical classroom profile. Remember this is an average picture of an average reader; there will be many exceptions.

Magazine #1: Profile

Most readers of Magazine #1 are 35 years or older. They are career professionals, probably male, with a minimum of four years university training. Disposable income is not a concern; maintaining the correct "image" is. These readers are likely to be corporate-climber yuppies. If they have children (many may choose not to), they have enough money to hire professional care to make their own life easier. They like luxury and are willing to pay for it. They probably read the magazine to get ideas for exotic vacations and the latest travel trends.

By now, some of you will be screaming Sexist! Stereotyping! Not politically correct!

And you're right. But for the purposes of this exercise, it's not only okay, it's important to look for stereotypes. Advertisers know they must make every penny of their budget count, so they will be looking at various venues for promoting their products using exactly these criteria.

A peak inside the covers of Magazine #2 will help illustrate this point from another angle. Here we find ads for:

- Hamburger Helper
- Kid's Ko-Op Kamping Gear
- Lego
- Quik Loss diet plan
- Harlequin romances

This profile implies a totally different type of reader. Here's the typical profile of Magazine #2's readership.

Magazine #2: Profile

Most readers will be female, between 20 and 40 years old. The majority will have no post-secondary education. Money, while not necessarily strangulation-tight, doesn't flow with nearly the abundance it does for Magazine #1's readers. Magazine #2's readers will likely read the magazine more for an escape into fantasy than for information about potential destinations to visit.

Now ask yourself the following two questions:

1. *What is the likelihood of Magazine #1 purchasing an article about budget family campgrounds along the Oregon coast?*

2. *What is the likelihood of Magazine #2 purchasing an article about a six-month, luxury tour of Russia and the Far East?*

While it isn't impossible, neither scenario is very likely without a truly unique and unobvious slant to the story.

Many people are amazed by the amount of information this simple exercise yields. Without even looking at a publication's stories and features, you have already formulated a good idea of who reads the magazine, and you can begin planning how an article can be slanted specifically to that readership.

The next step is to examine the rest of the magazine, section by section, so you can tighten your focus even further. Here are some specific questions you should research as you begin analyzing a potential market for your travel writing.

If you are targeting newspapers, you should consider these questions as well, but remember, most newspapers have less of a tightly focused readership.

(a) *What does the masthead say?* Usually located on the first four or five pages of the magazine, the masthead is where the names of editors, contributors, other personnel associated with the magazine, and all information about subscriptions and distribution is listed.

Check the titles of the writers closely. If most feature articles are written by staff writers, the magazine may be difficult to break into as a freelancer. On the other hand, if there are few or no staff writers listed and each issue features different authors in the masthead, this is an indication the publication probably relies heavily on freelancers for its material. You may have found a gold mine for your writing.

(b) *How long is the average feature article?* Although we've heard of publications that routinely request contributions of 4,000 words and then cut them back to 2,000 words or less, our advice is to submit articles of approximately the same length you see during your research. If most pieces run 1,000 to 1,200 words, find another market for your article of 4,000 words.

(c) *What tone is reflected in most articles?* Some publications want "facts only, please." Others prefer a folksy style, more like letters home to grandmum. Some want first person accounts, while others are interested only in the things "you will see, hear, and experience." Don't allow yourself to be lured into the trap of believing different is better when it comes to tone. Any knowledgeable editor knows the readers' decision to subscribe is based, in a large part, on the tone the magazine chooses to adopt.

(d) *Are the stories geared to people with or without children?* Life changes with children. Regardless of financial considerations, families, especially those with young children, have different needs and expectations about travel than those with only two adults and perhaps a pet to consider.

(e) *Is this primarily a publication for older or younger people?* As with children, age plays a major role in what readers expect. Be aware, however, that this does not mean that seniors are inactive compared to 20 year olds. Many seniors today are much fitter than their adult children. However, because they have a lifetime of experience behind them, they are often far more discriminating and want to learn about truly unique destinations and adventures.

(f) *What type of illustrations accompany most articles?* Are photos black and white or color? Are they wide, sweeping panoramas or tight shots of local people and their culture? Is the publication lavishly illustrated, with few words, or is the text more prominent than the artwork?

(g) *Are there aspects of travel the publication would be unlikely to publish?* Remember Magazine #1? This magazine is unlikely to accept anything about budget travel because its readers want luxury travel. Likewise, a publication geared to ski resorts is not a suitable market for an indepth study of how to enjoy desert camping.

(h) *What topics have been covered recently?* If the last two issues have covered the beaches of southern France and olive groves in Greece, it's unlikely the editor will be interested in these two subjects for several months, possibly longer.

Remember, though, that magazines often plan their editorial content months in advance. The rule of thumb is the bigger the publication, the further ahead they plan. Sometimes you will do all your homework, submit a scintillating idea you know is perfect for your target market, and still receive a polite rejection. Then you pick up the next issue and, to your horror, what do you discover? Someone else has written an article on exactly the same topic. As tough as it may seem, congratulate yourself. You obviously targeted exactly the right publication, you were just a couple of months too late, something not even the most experienced travel writer can always predict.

(i) *What themes recur?* Researching this question doesn't mean that you should avoid any topic similar to ones recently covered. If you discover in a general travel publication articles on the Champlain Air Museum (Mesa, Arizona), hot air ballooning in Australia, the Reno National Championship Air Races (Reno, Nevada), and the Abbotsford Air Show (Abbotsford, British Columbia) in four consecutive issues, you know something important about the editor. This person loves planes and flying.

How do you know that this is the editor's personal preference? A tight focus would be reflected in the title or mission statement of the magazine. For example, Field and Stream is a magazine obviously about hunting and fishing; writers should know to submit articles about hunting and fishing. Similarly, a title such as Air Adventures is a giveaway that the magazine wants flying stories. However, editors, like everyone else, have personal favorites, and sometimes these favorites show up subtly. In a general travel publication, it's often possible to see echoes of what those favorites are and use them to your advantage.

Turning back to our example, then, take your newfound knowledge and use it to work up an article idea with a unique slant. Perhaps there's a small but intriguing air museum near where you're planning your next vacation. Maybe there's a crusty old bush pilot who can tell you tales of flying the "Northern Route" and supply you with photos as well. Add in some up-to-date information about the place, and you have a story you already know the editor will at least be interested in on a personal level. It's a rare person who won't give even a marginally closer look to something he or she really likes. Even if your piece isn't accepted, he or she is more likely to remember a writer's name if that writer has sent in an article that touches the editor on a personal level.

Such painstaking inspection of a magazine may seem like time wasted, but most editors cite writers' lack of understanding about the needs of the specific publication as the most common reason for sending rejections slips. If you take the time to understand a magazine's needs, you are showing yourself as a writer with a professional attitude.

Sample #6 shows how one student analyzed a well-known travel magazine. By the time he was done, he'd realized his original idea for an article wouldn't work for this publication. He'd also come up with three brand-new ideas that would!

3. Don't forget about the foreign market

Remember the work you did in chapter 2 — gathering ideas from your own backyard? Here's where it can really pay off. One of the cheapest ways to break into print is to write about the area around your hometown and sell the article to an overseas newspaper or magazine. Research costs are minimal and overseas print media are always hungry for the new and different. You, as an overseas journalist, may add a touch of the exotic to their pages.

There are English-speaking countries all over the world, and English-language newspapers published in countries as unlikely as Samoa. A quick rule of thumb is that if the country was ever a British colony, or if it was occupied by British or American soldiers, it probably publishes English-language newspapers.

Writing for overseas newspapers differs a bit from writing for North American newspapers. You should use English a bit more formally than you would at home. Remember, foreign readers may be confused by idioms and slang that are commonplace at home.

Travel & Leisure (ads)

	Diamonds	Luxury Autos	Airlines	Cruise	Travel Destinations	Perfume	Watches	Computer, Camera, Video	Finance	Catalogue	Cigarettes
Issue 1		10	5	6	21	1	2	3	1	2	1
Issue 2	1	6	2	6	11		1	2			
Issue 3	1	5	3	4	15	2		3		1	2
Issue 4	1	8	3	5	7	2	6	2		1	1
Issue 5		9	4	3	24			2		1	
Issue 6	1	8	5	5	20	1	3	2		1	

A) *Travel & Leisure* magazine advertisements are targeted toward an American audience. The readers would be middle to upper middle class people, both male and female. They are most likely 35+ years old, white, well-educated professionals that either have no children, their children are grown or they have nanny to look after the children so they wouldn't be restricted in their travel. The readers most likely have a high disposable income and like the "good things" in life. The readers don't mind a little adventure but it must be achievable while doing it in luxury.

Ad sample lines:

Car ad:	"It suggests both Fortune 500 and Indianapolis 500"
Travel destination:	"Touch your dreams"
	"The ancient birthplace of good times"
Cruise:	"Is it possible that saltwater is an aphrodisiac?"
Perfume:	"The fragrance dreams are made of"
Airline:	"Comfort comes to a head."

B) *Travel & Leisure* magazine is geared toward providing travel destinations ideas to its readership. If the reader is an armchair traveler it could also be read for entertainment and general travel knowledge.

Courtesy of James Inglis.

C) The message the editor is hoping to instill is...hedonism is good. You've got money and I'm going to show you how to spend it.

D) Don't expect "New York on five dollars a day" in this magazine. This magazine is published by American Express Publications so thrift is not a focus. There is a "Best Deal" column but it couldn't be confused with a budget column. "Best Deal" talks about deals such as rooms at only US $209 per night and seven nights accommodation for only US $4,900.00.

This magazine would never discuss religion, government, or poverty. It is not interested in everyday life as an issue. The focus is on escape from that everyday life.

E) Sample Topics:

"The Best Small Hotels in New York"

"An Explorer in Genoa"

"South of France, North of Heaven"

"Sybil's Irish Country Drive"

"The Distant Shores of Corsica"

"Take me, Take my dogs"

"Where to go next"

"New York Nights"

"100 Great American Breakfasts"

The recurring themes for the articles are once again luxury and expensive travel destinations.

F) The "Ask T & L," "Best Deals," "Athletic Traveler," "Educations," "Food" department columns are staff written. The bulk of the magazine is set aside for articles. These articles do not appear to be staff written and the magazine does accept unsolicited submissions.

It also helps avoid some hilarious but embarrassing faux pas if you are already familiar with colloquialisms of the country you want to write for. In North America, for example, it's quite logical to put your suitcase in the *trunk* when you catch a *lift* to the airport with your neighbor. However, someone from Great Britain could be left shaking his or her head over why those crazy people in "the colonies" would put their suitcases in another container to go up the *elevator*. Of course, it would be perfectly logical to put them in the *boot* of their car for the ride to the airport.

Be on the look out for likely magazines and newspapers during your travels. Plan to spend a bit of time at a local magazine shop or library to pursue the names and addresses of likely prospects. We buy samples we can take home, instead of making copious notes. To save space and money, we photocopy the masthead whenever we can and order sample issues later. This means we're not burdened with heavy piles of paper right from the beginning of a long trip.

Your local library can also help. Two publications, *Ulrich's International Periodicals Directory* and *International Literary Marketplace*, are chock full of all kinds of overseas periodicals. They list hundreds of travel periodicals, as well as general interest magazines and newspapers interested in travel articles about North America. Reading through all the listings is a daunting task, but it's one that can pay off in big dollars to you.

Names and local events can cause confusion, too. Thanksgiving, the Orange Bowl, and a Polar Bear Swim (many readers who live no farther south from New York than Florida don't know what this annual New Year's Day event is) can be real head-scratchers for some overseas folks.

4. Writers guidelines and market listings

Part of any marketing plan includes studying the publication's writers' guidelines and market listings.

(a) Guidelines

There are virtually no magazines, regardless of size, that don't provide writers' guidelines to potential contributors.

Most newspapers, on the other hand, do not have guidelines, although a few of the very large newspapers do. It is best to read the actual newspaper to get an idea of what that paper is looking for.

Guidelines are a detailed summary of exactly what the editor and publisher wants and how much the magazine is willing to pay for it. However, the contents and format of writers' guidelines vary, from a conversational three or four paragraphs written in a casual style to several pages of precise information about content, photographic requirements, formatting, editorial preferences, and upcoming topics or themes. Sample #7 shows a typical, middle-of-the-road guideline.

Guidelines are free with an SASE (self-addressed, stamped envelope), and if you're writing for a sample in any case, why not request guidelines at the same time? This request does not need to be written in lyrical prose. If you set up a standard form on your computer, it is a just a matter of filling in the blanks, stuffing the letter into an envelope, and sending it off with correct postage. Or, you may prefer to photocopy 25 or 30 standard letters and fill in the blanks by hand. Either way, Sample #8 shows you just how simple a guideline request letter can be.

All publications change over time, so it's a good idea to date-stamp guidelines as they arrive. Don't worry about requesting new ones every year (that's what *Writer's Market* listings are for), but if you're basing a submission on guidelines that are five years old, it's worth a phone call to confirm —

- The publication is still in business

- The editor hasn't moved on, retired, or been replaced

- The publication's requirements (length, themes, style) are still the same

- The company still hangs its hat at the same address and hasn't moved uptown to the penthouse of a 100-story office tower

The most convenient way we've found to store guidelines is in a three-ring binder. It fits easily on the shelf, it's easy to update, and pages don't get lost or misfiled. All you need to do is invest in a set of alpha tabs and you're set. (The discussion of filing systems in chapter 16 discusses organizing your files in more detail.)

(b) Market listings

There are a host of excellent marketing books available in bookstores or in your library's reference section. These resources put the requirements and preferences of thousands of magazines at your fingertips. Some, like *Writer's Market*, published by Writer's Digest Books, are now also available on CD-ROM. See the Appendix for a more detailed listing.

Market listing books are closely related to guidelines. However, there are differences between the two, and we like to incorporate both into market research whenever possible.

Some of the more common differences are —

- Market listings usually give the editors' names; guidelines often don't.

Always include a SASE when requesting writers' guidelines. A standard #10 envelope (approximately 4" x 9" or 10 cm by 24 cm) is best. Smaller envelopes mean whoever sends the guidelines will have to struggle to stuff the paper in; larger envelopes waste postage money.

Market listings provide quick, up-to-date information on a publication's submission format, whether it likes new writers, if your name will be published with your article (a byline), pay rates, reader demographics, and sometimes useful tips from the editors.

Young Families Traveling Together

Young Families Traveling Together is a monthly magazine focusing on issues faced by families traveling with young children. Our aim is to encourage families to experience and learn from the wonders of the world around them. Our tone is lively and informative; our readers are inquisitive and expect to learn something new and exciting from every issue.

Young Families Traveling Together accepts unsolicited manuscripts, but gives preference to contributors who submit a query first. Please be sure to include an SASE (or SAE with IRCs [international reply coupons]) if you want a reply.

Feature articles: Our preferred length is 1,000 words, however we sometimes accept stories of up to 2,000 words. We need destination pieces which include information on activities suitable for the entire family to enjoy as a group. Special attention is paid to articles demonstrating "education with fun" and "cultural diversity is exciting" angles.

Inspirational and personal essays are always welcome, provided they aren't preachy.

Travel Tips and Tricks: New writers may find it easiest to break into the market by submitting personal anecdotes, unusual facts, news discoveries, and short travel humor to our Travel Tips department. Anything newsworthy is considered.

Photos: Photos will greatly enhance your chances of getting published with *Young Families Traveling Together*. State availability and format of any pictures you have when you first contact us, but do not send originals or negatives unless we request them. Photos must have captions indicating date, location, and subject, as well as model release forms if necessary.

Payment: We pay 5¢ to 10¢ per word on publication for feature articles. Payment for fillers and photographs is calculated on an individual basis.

123 Main Street
Big City, CA 90001
Phone: (646) 555-7777
Fax: (646) 555-4444

Janet Johns
456 Your Street
Your Town M8J 1J9

Dear Madame/Sir:

Would you please send me a copy of your writers' guidelines? I have enclosed a self-addressed, stamped envelope as requested. Thank you.

Sincerely,

Janet Johns

Janet Johns

Enclosure

- Market listings often state what percentage of a magazine's content is freelance-written; guidelines seldom include this information.

- Many market listings include a helpful tip from one or more of the publication's editors. These usually take the format of "things we really love to see" or "things we really hate to see." These are worth studying before you submit. Guidelines don't usually offer such tips.

- Market listings may not be current on the editorial slant of a publication, since listings are submitted by publications long before the book is published. Guidelines reflect such changes faster.

Not all magazines want their names listed in a marketing source book. Some editors feel that a writer who has taken the time to write for guidelines will be more likely to submit material appropriate to their needs than someone who has simply thumbed through a book. In some cases, listing in a writers' market book brings such a flood of submissions that the editor (who is more than likely already overworked) prefers to rely on the magazine's reputation to attract writers. Sample #9 shows a typical market listing.

(c) Newsletters, associations, and other info updates

Many association newsletters and magazines are specifically aimed at writers. Between us, we have subscriptions to at least a dozen, ranging from a four-page, double-sided newsletter printed at the local photocopier shop, to full-size, national circulation glossies. Although we certainly can't claim to read every word in every one, we do read most of the marketing information in most of the mail that comes through our office door.

The biggest advantage we find with these types of publications is that they are just about as current as you can get. There are listings about new markets, publications that have closed their doors, problem markets (usually related to payment and after all, isn't that part of what we, as writers, hope to gain from our writing?), and even contests and grants.

They also usually have some great ideas for improving your writing skills, as well as uplifting articles for those days when you wonder why you ever thought about getting into this crazy profession. Check the Appendix for a jump-start list.

Young Families Traveling Together

123 Main Street, Big City, CA 90001. Phone: (646) 555-7777 Fax: (646) 555-4444. Editor: Chief Cheese. 80% freelance written. Monthly magazine focusing on issues faced by young families including education, cultural issues, fitness, and financial challenges as they relate to travel. Responds in 10 weeks with SASE. Publishes an average of 6 months after acceptance. Byline given. Willing to work with new writers who show professionalism. Buys first rights. Buys 40–50 mss/year. Length 500–2,000 words. Pays 5–10¢ a word. Query first.

Non-fiction: General interest articles. We want upbeat pieces slanted toward the North American family with two or more children at home. Keep the tone lively but informative. Articles that concentrate on subjects to increase the quality of life and education for all family members always receive close attention. Humor, inspirational, and personal essay okay.

Fiction: Seldom use. Needs to be something very original for us to even consider it.

Fillers: Anecdotes, facts, newsbreaks, short humor. Buy 100–125 mss/year.

Tips: Submit new, fresh information concisely written and accurately researched. Our readers tend to be inquisitive about the world; don't underestimate them.

c. Step two: *learn to write a good query letter*

"Why should I write a query letter? Isn't it better to just send the whole manuscript so the editor can read it and decide on the spot if he or she wants to buy it?"

"My topic is really hot. If my query letter sits on the editor's desk for weeks, how will I ever get the article out before it's stale news?"

These are just two of the questions about queries many writers ask themselves at the beginning of their careers. But developing the ability to write a captivating query letter dramatically increases your chances of regular sales.

Do keep in mind, however, that although query letters to magazines usually get a reply, they almost never get a one from a newspaper. You will be better off sending the full article to a newspaper.

If you are targeting magazines, here's how to tap into this invaluable and necessary writing tool.

1. To query or not to query

In any profession, certain conventions always seem to be the instigators of intense controversy. In the writing profession, query letters (along with multiple submissions, discussed below in section **d.**) are one of those conventions.

Some schools of thought say you're wasting your time sending a query letter. Just write the article, submit it, and the publication will either buy it or it won't. Others claim that without a query letter, you've cut your chances by 50% or more. While the actual percentages are difficult to pinpoint, here are six good reasons to write a query letter before submitting your article.

(a) A well-written query gives the editor a chance to see a summary of your idea. With a 15-minute window of time and the choice of reviewing ten single-page query letters or ten five-page manuscripts, many editors faced with in-baskets measured in feet rather than inches will opt for compact query letters over full-length manuscripts. The queries are simply a more efficient use of their valuable and ever-limited time.

(b) A well-written query showcases your writing style and credentials in a single page. If you can capture an editor's attention in 400 words or less, you've demonstrated that you know how to write clean, concise prose.

(c) Editors like to have input into the format, length, and focus of an article. If you've spent days working up a tightly written feature of 3,000 words, it's horrifying to be told, "We love your article on the Grand Canyon. Please shorten it to 300 words and submit by..." Yes, it happened to one of us.

(d) Even if you've done a full market analysis, you can't know what is "in the pipeline" for upcoming issues. An editor may not be able to use your initial idea, but if he or she is impressed with your ability, a query letter can sometimes lead to other assignments.

(e) As crass and mercenary as it sounds, there is a financial consideration. A single-page query letter weighs less and is, therefore, less expensive to send (and return) than a complete manuscript. The difference between 50¢ postage each way and $1 each way may not seem like much at first glance, but when you're sending out 20 to 50 each month, it adds up fast. Ask any writer.

(f) It is okay to send query letters to a number of publishers at the same time. Section **d.** below discusses multiple submissions in more detail.

Some newspapers and magazines have restrictions on the kinds of sponsorships you can accept to do research. Refer to the guidelines to find out what the policy is.

If you are comfortable doing a telephone query, it may be well worth your time to do so. After pitching two or three well thought-out articles, you will start to develop a relationship with the editor. Your name will be more likely to come to mind when he or she is looking for someone to write a piece at short notice.

Make the time to attend press gatherings so you can meet editors — of both magazines and newspapers — face to face. It makes a big difference when an editor can put a name to a face. Relationships and the personal touch are important.

2. "Okay, give me five minutes and I'll whip off a couple of query letters"

So, you think you can whip off a couple of query letters in five minutes. Think again. Query letters are an important and time-consuming skill. Unless your idea is exceptionally complex, you have one page, and one page only, to give the editor the capsulized but still fascinating version of your idea, tell him or her why you are perfect to write about the idea you are presenting, and to ask for the sale.

(a) Use a catchy opening

Just like the article itself, a good query letter will have a catchy opening that hooks the reader. A useful but often overlooked tip is to use the opening sentence or paragraph of your query letter as the opening to your article. After all, if it has captured the editor's attention, it will most likely capture the readers' attention just as effectively. Of all the query letters we send out, more than 75% of those that are accepted have used this technique.

(b) Be in the right frame of mind when writing the query letter

There's a saying in many writing circles that most writers alternate between thinking what they've written is the most brilliant passage ever penned and thinking what they've written is the worst piece of garbage ever inflicted on the literate world. When you're writing your query letter, be sure you're in the first frame of mind.

If you have publishing credits, mention them. Perhaps you've been published in the local newspaper or an organization's newsletter. You may think it's "just a letter to the editor," but it's still a published credit. Perhaps you have special skills or indepth personal experience in an area. For example, who better to write about the tundra of the North than someone who has lived there for ten years?

(c) Explain why your article is suitable

Remember the writer who submitted a cruising article to a science fiction magazine? Clearly this person gave no thought to how the article would fit the publication's needs. If you can explain why your idea fits that publication's readership in a sentence or two, so much the better. It proves you've done your homework and read the magazine before submitting.

Your query letter is not an apology for being a writer, it's an offer to sell a product of value. Have confidence in yourself, and let that same confidence show through in your query letter.

(d) Never underestimate the importance of asking for the sale

Many students present some wonderful ideas, demonstrate they have the necessary background through either study or personal experience, and then fail to ask the editor to consider the article. Although most editors assume they are reading a query, it still leaves a question hanging about why this person bothered to write the letter in the first place. Maybe the writer is sharing the idea out of the goodness of his or her heart.

(e) This is an interview: look your best

If you were going to a job interview, would you wear ragged jeans, a dirty shirt, and neglect to tidy your hair? Doubtful. If you want the job, you'll be sure to do everything possible to make a good first impression. You'll dress well, speak clearly, and look the interviewer in the eye as you answer questions. Following standard business etiquette, you will also most likely shake hands when introduced and use the interviewer's name during conversation.

Body language is a powerful way to create a professional, competent image in someone's mind. In fact, studies show that approximately 90% of communication takes place through body language and tone of voice. Only 7% to 10% comes about because of the actual words used.

This puts writers at an immediate disadvantage. Writers, after all, have *only* their words to impress with. Since you've already lost most of the communication tools you would have in a face-to-face interview, you must make sure your query letter is brilliant: it is your first and often only way to make a favorable first impression with an editor. Before looking at queries in detail, here are a few quick tips to help make your first "meeting" a good one.

(a) Make sure your query is letter perfect. There should be no typos, spelling errors, or manual corrections. If something isn't right, reprint the page.

(b) Pay attention to layout and visual effect. Use standard business-letter format, a conventional font such as Times New Roman, Courier, or Garamond, and forget about fancy colored paper. Lime green paper with a curly-cue font may be fun for family letters, but it won't endear you to editors.

(c) Get the editor's name right and use it. If you're in doubt, invest 50¢ and call the publication to confirm spelling and gender. It's hard to maintain a sense of humor when you've just received your 210th letter addressed to Mr. Alex Meyers when you've been a woman all your life. (A friend of Susan's has been struggling with this for years.)

(d) Never fax or e-mail a query letter unless you've been invited to do so. Faxing not only uses up the publication's paper instead of yours (something all businesses object to), but a fax often takes much longer to get to the appropriate person. And while e-mail is becoming more common, it is still considered impolite to use this form of communication until you're so much in demand that editors are lining up outside your door waving contracts.

(e) Always enclose a SASE (self-addressed, stamped envelope). Always. If your target market is in another country, remember that its post office won't accept a SASE with stamps from your country. An American sending to a Canadian publication, for example, must find someone who will supply Canadian stamps.

An expensive alternative is to use IRCs, international reply coupons. IRCs cost up to seven or eight times the regular cost of stamps but are available, and redeemable, at any post office in any country — almost. We recently read about an editor of a trade journal who was unable to exchange IRCs in the small, southern Texas town where she worked. She eventually made the 150-mile (240 km) trip to the nearest major center, where she did find a post office that knew what they were, but she now tosses IRCs in the trash.

Remember also that Canada and the United States don't use the same measurement for weight. Pull out your calculator and brush up on converting between imperial measure and metric before laying out for postage.

d. Multiple submissions

Imagine someone saying to you, "I'm going to give you an all-expenses-paid trip anywhere in the world." Excited? We can't imagine what traveler wouldn't be. So how would you feel if the person making the offer suddenly came back with, "Oh sorry, didn't I tell you I also offered this to three other people? One of them has already taken me up on it. I've got only one trip to give out, so I guess you're out of luck."

If you are selling one-time serial rights, you could offer your article to several publications at the same time, whether or not their distribution areas overlapped, but most magazines wouldn't be interested; they aren't interested in being only one of three, four, or ten publications you've offered a particular article to. After all, why would they want to publish an article that's appearing at the same time in their nearest competitor's magazine? Not all will reject a multiple submission out of hand, but many will. This leaves you with the choice between sending a manuscript to only one place at a time and "neglecting" to mention it's a multiple submission.

Don't forget to include a SASE along with your one-page query letter and enclose a business card if you have one.

The first option is honest, but can keep your manuscript out of circulation for months while you wait to hear back from an overworked editor. The second is equivalent to playing Russian roulette with your reputation. If you are sending out an article to more than one magazine at a time, you must always indicate it is a multiple submission, no exceptions.

Query letters, on the other hand, can be sent out in batches of 5, 10, 50, or more. Why? Because you are offering a specific *idea*, not a specific article.

Let's say you've decided to write about a recent trip through the Canadian Rockies. You query a variety of magazines. One may be interested in the wildlife, another in the resorts and tourist attractions, and a third may request a detailed story about the building of the railway and its effect on the old mining towns along the route. With your notes and some research, one trip can easily accommodate all three requests.

e. How much are your articles worth?

1. Magazines

Magazines pay anywhere from nothing to several thousand dollars for travel stories. Obviously, rates will differ from one magazine to another. For example, some publications will pay by the word, others will pay a flat rate for an article.

You can expect a real price range in the compensation rates. *Condé Nast Traveler*, for example, pays $1 a word, expects articles to be 500 to 5,000 words, and pays the expenses of writers on assignment.

As another example, *Transitions Abroad* pays a flat fee of $75 to $150 for the lead article (up to 2,000 words), but more importantly for you, the editors there like to work with unpublished writers.

2. Newspapers

Newspaper journalism moves so fast that sometimes the first indication one of your articles has been published is when a check arrives on your doorstep. If you're lucky, an editor will contact you in advance to tell you the publication date for the article. Make sure you ask for a copy.

Newspapers pay anywhere from nothing to four or five hundred dollars for a several hundred word article. What they are willing to pay changes constantly. The vast majority of publications pay under $100 for a 500-word article.

The good news is that you are generally free to sell the same article to many different newspapers with little or no revisions. Most newspapers do not want a worldwide exclusive, but be sure to find out what rights they do want. (See chapter 18 to find out more about rights.)

The most important thing you must remember is not to sell the same article twice in the same readership area. It is okay to sell the same article to the *Chicago Sun Times* and the *San Francisco Chronicle*, but you'll have a problem if you also sell it to the *San Jose Mercury News* just down the coast from San Francisco. The two newspapers have a lot of readers in common. And none of the three regional newspapers would be happy to see the same article in *U.S.A Today*, which covers the whole country.

The best strategy is to select small- to medium-sized newspapers spread out around the continent. There are a lot of them, so you should be able to sell the same article several times in non-competitive areas. With a national newspaper, you can sell it only once.

3. Letter of assignment

A letter of assignment is simply a letter from an editor assigning a particular story to you. It means that, barring some unforeseen circumstance, the magazine *does* want to publish your article.

Not only does a letter of assignment give you some assurance you have a market for your article before you start spending time and money on research, but it is also useful for finding sponsors for your projects.

A letter of assignment is typed on the publication's letterhead and states terms of publication. It will confirm everything you have already discussed with an editor, including:

- Details of what the article will be about
- Ideas for titles
- Approximate length of the finished piece
- Photos to accompany the article
- Which issue the article is expected to appear in
- Deadline the finished piece must be submitted by

Sometimes these letters also state payment terms, including the kill fee if there is one, although many editors prefer to handle terms of payment in a separate letter. This also gives you a bit of privacy when you send copies of the assignment letter to sponsors.

Newspapers rarely hand out letters of assignment, but most magazines will. If the magazine you are writing for does not offer one, ask for it. Sample #10 shows an example of an assignment letter.

4. Follow through and follow up — politely

Your article is polished, formatted, and in the mail. Now you wait, and wait, and wait.... Sometimes it seems as if your manuscript has fallen into a black hole, never to be seen again. According to the writers' guidelines of the publication you sent it to, it responds in two months. But it's been ten weeks and not a word.

A **brief** (yes, you are hearing a heavy emphasis on the word), professional phone call is one option. Here are some things to remember before you begin dialing.

(a) Have all the details in front of you: when you sent the manuscript, its title, what subjects were covered, and, most important, the name of the editor you sent it to.

(b) Avoid the temptation to chitchat. This is, after all, a business phone call, not a social one.

(c) If the answer is no, accept it without arguing the point. However, if the editor sounds receptive, it's perfectly acceptable to ask what you could have done to make your submission better suited to the publication's needs.

(d) Remember, editors are human. They have off days just like the rest of us. If the person you are speaking with sounds brisk or answers in curt monosyllables only, it probably has nothing to do with you or your writing abilities and everything to do with the pressures of getting a magazine out on time.

Even if you are uncomfortable doing queries over the telephone, you can increase your chances of getting published by calling the editor after you send in the article. It may be a little more expensive to call, but it's guaranteed to be faster than waiting for return mail. Phone calls are also more personal; they open doors better than letters or faxes.

Another course of action, one many writers find effective, is to send a manuscript status form. These forms make it convenient for the editor to respond and also show that you are a serious writer who is concerned about prompt turnaround. In some cases, these

Let's Travel
459 Good Street
Theirtown, LZ 56987

January 15, 199-

Ashley Smith
123 Main Street
Anytown, BC X5V 3Y7

Dear Ashley:

This letter is to confirm your assignment for the May 199- issue of *Let's Travel* magazine, which is devoted to romance and travel.

Your article suggestion, "Sailing the 'Sundays," on cruising throughout the various islands of the Whitsundays in Australia will work beautifully with our editorial calendar. Please advise of the exact details of the trip as early as possible.

As we discussed, the article should be approximately 1,500 words in length, with photographs to accompany the text. Your deadline is March 30, 199-.

The contract will be sent to you separately.

Sincerely,

Lindsey Black

Lindsey Black
Managing Editor

forms have been known to prompt an acceptance! Sample #11 shows a form used successfully by one writer to track his many submissions to various markets.

5. A note on editing

Newspaper editors need a lot of material every day, and while they need to get the product out quickly, they also have stringent restrictions on space and style requirements. Don't expect to be consulted about changes to your article. In the world of newspapers, most editors simply don't have the time.

Magazine editors have a certain amount of lead time to work with, and are slightly more likely to let you know about proposed changes. Some (although not many) will even send you a copy of the edited article long before publication. However, to avoid disappointment and wasted frustration, don't expect that you will be asked.

Your chances of having input about changes to your writing increase the longer you have worked with a given publication. But even long-time pros must occasionally close their eyes to butchered paragraphs.

Despite what some people would like you to believe, there are literally thousands of markets for your travel articles. While each market has its own idiosyncrasies, by now you should have a good feel for how to search out those markets best suited to your writing style and interests. And for those of you considering the book market, the next two chapters are just for you!

Dear Mr. Aircraft:

I am writing about two stories I sent you last November. I'd like to pursue alternative markets for both these pieces if you don't have them under active consideration for publication.

For your convenience, here is a check-off form to help me determine the status of these stories. Thank you for returning it promptly.

On _____ I submitted for your consideration a ms/s called: _____. I have not heard from you regarding its/their status. Would you please (X) the appropriate place(s) in the list below and return this convenient form to me in the enclosed SASE. It will help with tracking/evaluating/marketing my submissions.

( ) *If* we received your manuscript, we have no record of such.

( ) You included no SASE or one with insufficient postage.

( ) We do not read or return unsolicited mss (SASE or not).

( ) Your story is still under consideration.

( ) Your story is on file for possible future use.

( ) Your story was/will be printed in the _____ issue.

( ) We may have mislaid your ms. Please resubmit.

( ) The following reason:_____

_____.

With appreciation,

Mr. Professional Writer

Courtesy of Arthur G. White.

10
Publishing your first book

Most travel writers eventually think about writing a book. Many think it is the road to wealth. We admit that when we started, we assumed if our book did well, we would be half way to retirement.

The reality is that most travel books are not best-seller material. You won't sell a million copies a year. Count on it NOT reaching the *New York Times* best-seller list. Even if your book does better than 99% of the travel books out there, you will not retire on the royalties from your tome.

In addition, writers on average are paid $1.00 to $1.50, or less, for every book sold. After you deduct expenses for research, including your travel costs, it's difficult to make a profit.

Still, it is alluring and rewarding. There is the prestige of being an author, and if you like to write and travel, it's fun work. And there's always the chance *your* book will be a high-volume seller for decades. A few thousand dollars extra each year adds up to great pay over time.

a. The commercial hook

To an editor, the most convincing argument in favor of your book is the commercial appeal. Hooking editors with several well-thought-out marketing strategies is a better bet than trying to impress them with your witty writing. Editors want to know who this book will appeal to and how to capture their attention.

The best hooks or angles can be summarized in a phrase that works as a title. "The Big Nose Guide to the Wineries of Europe" or "Love and Sex in the Greek Isles — The Over Thirty Guide to Night Clubs, Beaches, and Other Attractions," have a definable theme that suggests who the publisher might aim for. If you have concrete ideas about who these potential buyers are and how to reach them, editors and publishers will take your proposal much more seriously.

As an example, one writer showed how her books could be sold to travel agents to use as gifts for their clients. Another compiled information on the cruise industry so it appealed to both the general reader who would purchase the book in bookstores and to school counselors as an educational tool for students who want to go into the cruise industry.

Actively think about the money-making possibilities from the very beginning of your book project. Consider these questions:

(a) Which countries can this book be sold in? Is there a potential for the publisher to sell foreign rights? One author we know makes far more money from sales of foreign rights than from sales in her homeland.

(b) Can you describe the demographics of the people you want to read this book? What age range would it appeal to? Where do they shop? What do they buy? How much money do they have? Do they have children or pets? All of these details give the publisher grist for their marketing.

(c) Are there distinctive characteristics of the group who would read the book? The wine title above, for instance, might be sold in wine stores as well as bookstores where wine aficionados congregate.

(d) Can the book be used as a premium? A guidebook on Hawaii might be used as a free gift for anyone booking a trip to Hawaii through a tour operator.

A habit of close attention to the commercial aspects of any project from the outset will dramatically increase your chances of being published.

1. Do your homework

When you are looking for a publisher for your book, your first step should be to go to the bookstore and library to see who is publishing the kind of book you would like to write yourself. The lead time in publishing a book can be so long, it is vital you have the most up-to-date information you can about any potential publisher's focus.

Frankly, we found it a little embarrassing to be going through all the travel books in a bookstore and writing down the publishers' names, but the books were more available than in the library where they always seemed to be checked out.

While you are at the bookstore, make a list of the trim size (the physical dimensions) of each book, the number of pages, and the kinds of covers they have. This will be useful for your proposal. Note any titles whose theme is similar to yours.

But don't ignore your library as an excellent source of information. The librarian will be able to direct you to a number of different reference manuals which list most books in print. You won't be able to examine the physical book as you can in a bookstore, but it will give you book titles.

When you go to book fairs, take a sturdy satchel with a shoulder strap or a small backpack for your prizes. Three or four hours of heavy plastic bags cutting your hands is torture you can do without.

When our research reveals a likely publisher, we call or write to order its most recent catalogue. We keep these in a pile in our office and use them for reference. We jump at every opportunity to go to booksellers' conferences, too. It is a great place to pick up the latest catalogues from several companies quickly.

Once you have found the publishers of your kind of book, look them up in the *Writer's Market*. There you'll find all the information you need about each one, including:

(a) Address

(b) Telephone and fax numbers

(c) E-mail address

(d) Name of the submissions editor

(e) Compensation rate

(f) Details on what it is looking for in manuscripts

(g) Whether it takes unagented submissions and/or multiple submissions

(h) How it wants queries and submissions made

(i) How long a response to inquiries takes

(j) How many books it publishes per year

Be careful about paying agents an up-front "reading" fee. Some "agents" charge a small (or sometimes not so small) fee for reading your manuscript. Supposedly, this is to assess whether they want to take it on. It is not customary for reputable agents to charge reading fees.

Many will also list helpful insider tips and other useful information. The listings in the directory are "based on editorial questionnaires and interviews," so you can have some confidence in the information's accuracy. We have found this to be an invaluable time saver.

If you decide to use an agent, you'll discover that finding one to take you on can be as hard as finding a publisher. Many publishers rely on agents to cull the good from the irrelevant. They will look at a manuscript or proposal sent by an agent, but if it is badly written or completely out of the realm of what the company publishes, the agent's reputation, not yours, takes a nose dive. A couple of bad manuscripts and the agent goes from being an asset to an irritation. This makes agents necessarily cautious about what they take on.

Many agents nowadays are willing only to help negotiate a contract once you have managed to acquire one. Frankly, an entertainment lawyer can do the same and only charge you a single, flat rate instead of taking 15% of your royalties for the rest of the book's life.

For some writers, the worst part of having an agent is waiting for them to find a publisher for you. This passive stance can have a frustrating and discouraging effect. You feel out of touch with what's happening to your book.

Fortunately, very few travel publishers refuse to look at unagented work. But if after doing your research, you feel your only choice is to go after one of the big publishing houses that accepts only agented work, you're stuck. Head to the library or your favorite bookstore and get a copy of *Guide to Literary Agents* (see the Appendix for more details).

If you do find an agent who agrees to take on your project, it is essential you check out his or her reputation thoroughly. When you have an agent, the royalty cheque is normally paid to the agent, who then pays you. Some authors report they have problems getting paid. In the worst cases, they never see a dime.

A more common complaint, that reference checking will usually reveal, is the agent's lack of effort and communication with their clients. This is not only frustrating, but can mean delays measured in years in getting your book to a publisher.

Before you hire an agent, request references and check them all. You cannot afford to be shy about this. Call everyone on the list. That's right, phone every single one. Do not sign any contract with an agent without checking his or her performance with everyone you can. It's your career — or lack of one — that's in the balance.

As a last step, always talk to a lawyer about any contract you are asked to sign.

b. The telequery

Publishing houses say you should send a query letter before you send a proposal. We tried that. Some publishers took six months before they told us they would or would not like to see a proposal.

Questions to ask an agent's reference

- How well did the agent do for you?
- Is the agent still representing you? If not, why not?
- Would you recommend working with this agent?
- Did the agent keep you advised of all developments?
- Did the agent give you feedback about your proposal or manuscript?
- Was there a plan for marketing your manuscript to publishers or was the effort ad hoc?
- Is there anyone else you think I should speak with who might give me some insight into this agent?
- What percentage did the agent earn? (You'd be surprised how many people will tell you everything you want to know including all the financial details. Most authors want to help fellow authors.)
- Did the agent pay on time?

We find that with one brief call to the acquisitions editor, we can get a sense of whether the title we are contemplating is something that publisher would be interested in.

This is guaranteed to be frustrating. Nowadays, voice mail doesn't even let you desperately question the receptionist when you can't get through to the editor. But persistence can occasionally bring you a crucial piece of advice or encouragement.

Before you call, you should research what the publisher's newest titles are. (Check with bookstores or get the information from the publishing house directly.) This will give you a feel for its marketing thrust as it was six months to a year ago, when the books were contracted. Although the house may have changed its title mix in the interim — sometimes dramatically — you at least have some background information to use in your conversation with the editor.

c. The book proposal

Every book starts with a book proposal. If the editor is your uncle, it might be a short conversation over breakfast, but the book still starts with a proposal. Whether it's Uncle George or an editor you don't know, all proposals have basically the same aim and format. They must convey an indepth look at the project and the author. No matter how gussied up they are — pink paper and ribbons — if they don't accomplish those objectives, the book will be rejected.

The good news is that by the time you finish your proposal, your book is partly written. All proposals include these items:

(a) A bio (see chapter 13 for a discussion of bios)

(b) Sample chapters, usually three to five

(c) An outline

(d) Notes on marketing strategy

(e) Any backup or supporting material that might shed light on the book

Every proposal is different, so don't feel constrained by what you read here. As long as you present the information in a coherent and organized fashion, just about anything is okay.

1. The cover letter

The cover letter is a very brief summary of what you have in mind and a bit of information about you. Use the best opener or hook you can write. Put pizzazz into your opening, but don't make wild, unsubstantiated claims. Don't, for instance, write that this is the best book since *Around the World in 80 Days*. Editors have enough experience to tell if there is a reasonable chance for success as long as you give them enough information to make a informed decision.

Concentrate on giving the highlights in a very abbreviated form. The cover letter should not be more than a page except in the most unusual circumstances. It should never be more than two pages, even if you really have just completed the best book since *Around the World in 80 Days*.

2. Title page

Include the working title and your name, address, and phone number. That's it. See chapter 8 for details on manuscript presentation.

3. Introduction

The introduction should highlight the book's concept and its strongest features.

4. The author

Tell the editor why you are qualified to write this book. Overcome your innate modesty by talking about yourself in the third person. If you have a particularly long but relevant bio, include it in summarized format under a separate heading.

5. Physical characteristics

Be assertive. You are painting a picture so a potential publisher can mentally hold your book in their hands. It doesn't matter that it will end up a different size than you visualize or that the title will be different or even that the pictures you think are perfect have been replaced by something else. This exercise will also help *you* see the finished product. You may discover the number of words you think it will take means the book is four times as thick as any other book on the shelf. Time to cut some. Here are the main points to think about.

(a) How many pages will it be?

(b) Will there be pictures and illustrations? Remember, color increases the cost of the book while black and whites or drawings are cheap to reproduce.

(c) What are the dimensions you envision? The standard size is 9" x 6". The more a book deviates from this, the harder it is to sell to bookstores.

(d) What lists, addresses, appendixes, or indexes will be included?

The quickest way to estimate the number of words is to find a book of similar size and type. Count ten lines of words and average the number of words per line. Next, count the number of lines per page and multiply it by the average number of words per line to find a per page estimate. Divide this into the number of words you estimate are needed to cover your subject and you'll have a reasonably reliable estimate of your total projected page count.

(e) Are there unusual aspects of the book that will make it unique in the marketplace?

Complete this section of the proposal after you have finished your outline so you know how many words you need to write. (See the sidebar for details on how to quickly estimate the number of words in your manuscript.)

6. Marketing

Who does this book appeal to? Backpackers? Ecotourists? Seniors? Demographic statistics should be presented here to give the marketing department some idea who will buy your book.

If you know where the publisher can sell a whack of books, this is the place to let them know. For example,

> Bulk sales of *From Wagon Wheels to Third Wheels* to the American Automobile Association and several state tourism boards should be explored, since this scenic highway meanders for hundreds of miles through several states.

You should also mention if the book can be sold in other countries, publicity opportunities (known as "forewords") written by famous people, and any time restrictions that need to be considered. Can this book go to market anytime or is there a deadline of some sort? Let the publisher know up front to avoid problems later.

7. Completion date

If you must do two months research in Fiji and you can't leave until after the December holidays, don't promise to have the manuscript ready whenever the publisher wants it — it may be too soon. Again, be specific and be sure you can do what you say you can do. There is no point in promising a two month turnaround if you haven't even started on the manuscript.

8. Competition

It is very important to research other books. Are there other books covering the same material? If so, how is your book different? Your librarian (marry one if you can) will help track down books with a similar theme. If you overlook a popular book the editor knows about, you'll damage your credibility.

Include some idea of how well covered the subject is in other media. If it is already available in several dozen formats, from books to videos, you'll have to explain what your proposed book will add. The whales of Baja are mentioned in every guidebook of the peninsula, and several documentaries have been created about the area. Your book has to say something different.

9. The outline

Although we've seen handwritten, single-page outlines that got book contracts, we don't recommend quite that much brevity. Outlines should be almost a point form precis of what is in each chapter. Although not a paragraph by paragraph summary, it must cover all the main ideas.

Start each chapter with the title and a first sentence stating the main theme of the chapter. Then, in concise and cogent writing, tell the editor exactly how you are going to support the theme.

10. Sample chapters

Most editors want to see a couple of sample chapters to see how you write and how you intend to handle your subject. They want to see your organization and a sample of the tone you will use. Don't pick the two-page introductory chapter for your sample. Choose something that really shows what you can do. Work these chapters over until they are the best you have ever written.

11. Formatting your proposal

The time to let your creativity show through is in your writing, not the way you format a proposal. In chapter 8, you'll find guidelines to help you make your proposal as visually appealing as possible. This is one time when being different is not a desirable characteristic. Stick with the format editors and publishers expect.

12. Mailing your proposal

Include backup material if it is brief and relevant. Resist the temptation to send everything. Never send originals of anything. If copies are lost in the mail (yes, it does happen), they can be replaced. Short of returning to the wilds of Arabia, originals can't.

We recommend sending disposable copies, rather than including postage to have the proposals returned to you. It's easier to make new copies, and our experience is that some copies are not mailed back, even though a self-addressed stamped envelope with correct postage was included. Proposals that do come back are sometimes marked up, dog eared, and missing chunks.

Some editors will not touch a subject or destination that has recently had unfavorable news coverage. More than one manuscript has been shelved because of a completely unrelated upheaval or crime spree in the country the book is about.

If this happens to you, wait for a change in the circumstances and then submit. In the meantime, move on to something else.

If you do want your material returned, and you are sending to a foreign country, remember your return postage must be in that country's stamps. U.S. stamps will not work for an editor who is situated in France. Chapter 9 discusses IRCs (international reply coupons).

It's a professional gesture and will ease your anticipation a bit if you enclose a stamped postcard or reply form (see Sample #11 in the previous chapter) addressed to yourself which the editor can drop in the mail. Since most editors don't have the time to call, you'll at least know the proposal arrived safely.

13. Multiple submissions

Submitting your proposal to more than one publishing house only makes sense. Since most houses take six months or more, it could take literally years to find the right house if you mail your proposal sequentially, one at a time to your list of potential publishers.

On the other hand, publishers don't want to evaluate your proposal, take the time to pitch it to their colleagues, work out the numbers, and draw up a contract, only to find the book is coming out next spring with a competitor.

We have a lot of sympathy for this position but can't justify their approach. However, it is an industry standard to let a publisher know others are looking at it. If you are submitting simultaneously to several houses, a simple "This proposal is being submitted to several other publishing companies" in the cover letter is fair warning.

d. Writing guidebooks

It seems no one travels anywhere without a guidebook tucked in his or her pocket. Sit on an art gallery's steps in Europe or hike a trail in British Columbia and someone will pull out a guide to discovering the wonders of the area.

There are guidebooks that tell you how to find a bed in a region's best châteaus or where to find crystals in a particular valley. Guides cover travelers' every taste, from bike trails and ski resorts to restaurants and hotels.

Guidebook writing is an expanding market because these books provide real value for the reader. They forewarn travelers of problems, highlight points of interest which would be easily missed, and

---

If you regularly send proposals to other countries, get in touch with someone in that country who is willing to send you stamps. Look for contacts among your friends, relatives, travel organizations, writing groups, or even school alumni. Someone will eventually help you out.

Prescription for getting an editor to read your book

1. Go to bookstores and libraries to research publishers that publish your kind of book.

2. Come up with an angle or commercial hook and condense it down to a catchy title.

3. Call the publishing house and ask for the name and official title of the acquisitions editor.

4. Pitch your idea over the phone to see if the editor is interested in seeing your proposal. Alternately, mail a query letter (don't fax it unless the editor has specifically requested it).

5. Write a proposal.

6. Have someone edit your proposal. Polish it until it is the best it can possibly be.

7. Follow up with a phone call a month or two later to see what happened with your proposal.

objectively look behind the advertising puffery of tourist boards, hotels, and eateries. After a few hours of reading, the traveler can have a rudimentary grasp of the people and politics of a region, something that might otherwise take weeks to discover.

It takes a special breed to write guidebooks. While writers of promotional pieces for a destination can engineer a restful vacation, guidebook writers never have that luxury. As Christopher Baker, author of five popular guidebooks and contributor to several others, says, "Guidebooks are a real labor of love."

He should know. His royalty-earning guide to Cuba (Moon Publications) took two years and thousands of hours to compile. And although he was paid "very well" for his guide to Jamaica (Lonely Planet), when you question him closely, you discover on an hourly basis, he still barely made minimum wage.

Several guidebook writers also admit it takes a toll on their social life. It's hard to keep up with friends, lovers, and spouses when you spend months away doing research. To balance this downside, it helps to have a fascination with the subject and a dedication to exploring every nook and cranny for your readers.

Guidebook writing is still a growing market. If you want such a career, there is room for you. Existing publishers are constantly expanding their list of titles or beginning new ones. They are looking for ideas. Before you jump in, here are some things you should know:

(a) Writing guidebooks can be lucrative compared to other travel books. Publisher's royalties have been known to be as high as 18%, but the average is around 10% of net.

(b) The trend is to pay writers a flat fee to research and write all or parts of the book, or to purchase a manuscript outright. At the upper end of the scale, earnings of US $35,000 to US $40,000 are not unheard of for one book.

(c) Many publishers do pay an advance to cover the cost of research, as much as $10,000. However, even $10,000 doesn't go very far, and many writers report they dig into their own pocket before the project is finished.

(d) Publishers usually hire the same person to do updates for a fee. When these writers retire or change to another field, the publisher goes looking for someone to refresh the book. Being at the right place at the right time can play a big part in being hired for one of these jobs. One natural history guide publisher spreads the word at rock climbing stores! Naturally, writers who come with good recommendations or who have worked successfully with an editor before are chosen first.

(e) One very big advantage is you do not need to market yourself as tenaciously as you do as a freelance magazine or newspaper writer. The more you do, however, the better known you become to guidebook editors and publishers. Eventually, projects come looking for you.

(f) If you take on writing an objective-evaluation type of guidebook, you may not be able to accept any free travel. The publisher may require a detailed description of what you have accepted before agreeing to publish your work.

(g) Politics can play havoc with your income, so when choosing a subject, research the area carefully. One civil war can ruin your royalties for years. Sales for guidebooks to Bosnia, for example, only appeal to a few really jaded travelers.

(h) It is likely you will need to take photos and produce maps for your guide. Some publishers may require samples of your photography to be submitted with your proposal.

(i) Be creative. There are more ideas for guidebooks than there are countries or regions. If you have a hobby, is there a guide to the hot spots for your favorite pastime? How about a guide to lost mines which features the history of each mine, the best way to travel there, where to stay, where to eat, and what to see.

The easiest way to find out who publishes guidebooks is to go to a major bookstore and look over the selection. Check under travel, history (historical guides), recreation (hiking, biking, canoeing) and the natural earth sciences (mineral and geological formation guides). Also have a look at *Writer's Market*.

e. Negotiating the contract

Good grief! It's a thick envelope from a publisher, and it's not your manuscript being returned! If you can faint now, please do. It is essential you harness your excitement as quickly as possible. Better yet, save it to wax your car or put a new addition on your house. Right now, there's work to do!

First, find a lawyer well versed in publishing law who can help you with the legal details. Don't use your Uncle Jake or your regular family lawyer. You need someone who deals with publishing issues everyday and understands the nuances.

Use your lawyer as a resource and a second, smarter pair of eyes, especially when things are complicated. Have your lawyer review your contract, but don't automatically use him or her to negotiate a contract. At $150 and up an hour, legal fees can soon eat into any possible extra earnings you as a first-time author might gain.

We're in favor of doing your own contract negotiating in most cases. When you're finished, you'll have received a good education, feel a sense of accomplishment, and most likely have saved enough money to throw a party.

More to the point, your first book contract is probably a take-it or leave-it offer from the publishing house. It knows the compensation it is giving you is your entrée into the world of published authors and are unlikely to bend much. There probably won't be much you can do, but for the sake of experience, try to negotiate a couple of minor points anyway.

This does not mean you should go without advice. If you have never read a contract, you will need someone to explain what the various terms and conditions are about. Call a local magazine or book association, legal referral service, or another published author for the name of a lawyer who can tell you about the parts of the contract you don't understand. We try to figure out everything we can before calling for the lawyer — and the big legal invoice.

It is highly unlikely you will receive an advance for your first book. Remember, an advance is a draw against royalties, and publishers are generally unwilling to gamble on what your first book will earn. In the end, you'll receive the same money with or without the advance. It does, however, help defray the cost of up-front research, and for some writers this is a big consideration. If the publisher decides not to publish your book, you'll probably be able to keep the advance as a consolation.

Occasionally a publisher will contract for a book and then decide it does not want to publish it. Most contracts have a clause that lets the publisher out of its obligation to actually print and distribute the book without penalty. Although this could happen to you, it is unlikely. Publishers know their business and won't go to the effort of negotiating a contract if they aren't serious about publishing it.

f. Royalties

Royalties are usually a percentage of the net revenues to the publisher or a percentage of the retail price of the book.

Most publishers calculate your share on the basis of the retail cover price of the book — 5% of $15 is pretty straightforward.

Net means your share is calculated after payment to middle people, like distributors or wholesalers and the retail bookstores, is subtracted. A retailer usually gets 40% to 50% of the cover price for selling the book. On a $15 book, it may make as much as $7.50. If there is a distributor or other wholesaler handling the book for the publisher, it usually takes 10% to 15% of the cover price. $7.50 for the retailer and $2.25 for the distributor leaves $5.25 for the publisher.

Both methods should yield about the same money to you. 10% to 15% of the net is approximately the same as 6% of the gross retail selling price. On a $15 book with 40% and 15% paid out to middle people, your royalty will be $0.53 to $0.79, depending on whether you get 10% or 15% of the net. The same book at 4.5% to 6.5% royalty on the gross retail price yields about the same cash.

The only advantage of a percentage based on the retail price is that it's easier to understand.

Writer's Market can give you information on what publishers are willing to pay. For example, in "Writer's Market," Globe Pequot Press, publisher of travel guidebooks, is listed as making an outright purchase, or paying 7½% to 10% royalty on the net price of a book. It also offers an advance.

g. *The indemnity clause*

All publishing contracts have indemnity clauses. Basically, you promise the work is yours and original. If it later comes out you didn't get the right permissions for a photo or you libeled someone, the publisher can look to you for payment of the legal fees, as well as for reimbursement for any money it has to pay out because of your mistake.

This clause will not go away, no matter how much you push to have it altered. And rightfully so. The publisher has to depend on you to do your research correctly. The best defense against problems is to make sure you do your job right.

If you are really worried, talk to your lawyer about putting everything you own in a friend's name. Then you can worry about what your friend is going to do with your assets instead.

As a final word, read *The Novel* by James A. Michener. Although a fictional account of a novelist's career, it is probably a barely disguised autobiography. Sometimes there is more truth in fiction than in nonfiction. In the novel, Michener takes you through all the stages of a book's life. Most important, he gives you a feel for what goes on in the minds of editors, agents, and publishers. When you are talking to an editor on the phone, you'll be able to "see" all the piles of competing manuscripts in their office.

h. Self-publishing

We do not recommend publishing a book yourself if this is your first foray into travel writing. Still, we suspect publishing your own travel tales will be the first effort for some of you. If you survive financially, you will have learned a great deal in a short amount of time about the business of writing and selling travel.

Here are some tips we have gathered by watching others self-publish. They are worth remembering.

1. Know how you are going to market your book

Spend as much time on sales planning as you do on the book's creation. One self-publisher likened self-publishing to raising a child. Conception to birth is a nine-month process. Getting the book to a profitable niche is like raising it and putting it through college. If the book idea doesn't have a thorough marketing plan with multiple means of selling copies, you are going to lose a lot of money.

In a real sense, your printed masterpiece is invisible. Unless you are willing to spend countless hours shoving your book in the marketplace's face, self-publishing is not for you.

2. Do a small press run — no more than 3,000

Do a small press run no more than 3,000, or, preferably, even smaller. As one writer who did a press run of 10,000 said, "I have enough books left to fully insulate my garage." It is rare to sell 5,000 copies of a self-published first print run.

3. Read, and talk to anyone who works in publishing

There are several good books on the subject of self-publishing that you should be able to find in your local library. Here are three we've found worth looking at:

(a) Marion Crook and Nancy Wise's *How to Self Publish and Make Money*, published by Westwood Creative Artists.

(b) John Kremer's *1001 Ways to Market Your Books*, published by Open Horizon.

(c) Barbara Gaughen and Ernest Weckbaugh's *Book Blitz, Getting Your Book in the News,* published by Best Seller Books.

4. Stay away from updates

Try to minimize time-sensitive information. Travel writing usually has a lot of contact information, names, and addresses which go out of date as companies move or fold. The more you put in, the faster the book becomes obsolete and the faster you are forced to dispose of them or print another edition.

5. Consider whether self-publishing will leave you fulfilled

Self-publishing their first book leaves many authors unfulfilled. Self-publishing is slowly gaining recognition as a viable means of publicizing your work. Still, self-published books do not have the same cachet as books published by an established publishing house. With some remarkable exceptions, self-published authors do not normally garner the same respect as authors published by other houses.

i. Vanity publishing

Maybe you have seen those ads in the backs of some writers' magazines promising a complete book from design to marketing at rock-bottom prices. Yes, these companies want you to pay them to publish your book.

Absolutely, positively, do not get lured into vanity publishing. Despite how easy the ads and salespeople make it sound, you won't make a million dollars. The sales that vanity publishers promise rarely materialize. Sure, they put out a press release, but everyone who receives it already knows what that publisher's business is and never takes its offerings seriously. Technically, vanity publishers will fulfill their end of the bargain, but you probably won't break even on sales, and many writers have lost a substantial amount of money.

Editors and sponsors also feel a vanity book marks you as a dabbler, someone not to be taken seriously. The equation seems to be that if you had to pay to have your material published, you must not be a very good writer. Vanity publishers are ideal for putting together a small print run of a book on your family tree, but not as a career-enhancing move.

11

Wringing the most out of your book

Royalties from one book generally won't provide you with a decent living. We estimate we made about 25¢ an hour from the royalties on our first book.

Many first-time authors who discover this appalling fact never write a second book. Once through the grinder without adequate pay is enough. This attitude is so common in the industry that there is a phrase for authors with only one title: the one-book wonder. Some professional organizations do not even recognize you as a professional writer unless you have written two or more books. For example, the American Society of Travel Writers requires that you have two books to your name to join its club.

Here are some suggestions for squeezing all you can from your book, whether it's your first and only book or your fiftieth:

a. Ask for marketing support

Try to obtain a commitment from the publisher to support your book with marketing money. At a minimum, it should be willing to send out press releases and follow up by phone on your behalf.

Many publishers subscribe to the "throw them up in the air and see which ones fly on their own" theory of promotion. Those books that generate some interest get promotion money. Those that don't, die a quiet commercial death.

As an alternative, do your own public relations. Have the publisher provide you with advertising and marketing materials, as well as a small budget to cover postage. It should at least give you a nicely designed, all-purpose handout. Book covers are too expensive for you to duplicate on your own, but the publisher can print extras for you very cheaply. Be sure to ask for some ahead of time.

Marketing support is worth more than arguing about a slightly better percentage point on your royalty, especially for your first book. Publishers are also more likely to consider additional marketing than pay you more cash. After all, if more books sell, both you and the publisher will make more money in the end anyway.

b. Write a series

Look for ways to turn your book into a series. Why stop with the best restaurants of California? There are 49 sequels from the United States alone, then 10 more if you include the provinces of Canada. And you haven't even left North America yet!

Could your book become a series?

Publishers love series. If the first one sells well, they have a built-in readership for subsequent volumes. Their marketing efforts for the first book spill over to the second. Instead of starting from scratch as they would have to with a new book, they can adjust their efforts to take advantage of promotions that worked with the last book in the series. Each subsequent book adds to the reputation and luster of the whole series.

Finding new authors and new books with commercial potential is an arduous, expensive, and time-consuming task. Editors will be tickled not to have to find another untried author with an untried concept.

c. Offer updates

If your book is going to have a lot of contact information, and the majority of travel books do, you need to be aware of the pros and cons of new editions to update your work. If you have a fast seller, a few revisions each edition is not a problem for most publishers. But if your book languishes on the shelf, it will slowly go out of date. Addresses and phone numbers will develop enough inaccuracies to become a problem for readers, and a bad reputation follows swiftly. Long before that happens, your publisher will have remaindered your books through a discount bookstore.

Publishers seem to be split on the idea of a book that needs a new edition each year to update information. Some like the idea that once they have established a market, the same customers will be looking for the updated edition year after year.

On the other hand, publishers must determine the number of books to print much more carefully. If they overestimate the demand, they end up with unsalable books. If they underestimate, chances are by the time they realize the book is a sell out, they won't have enough time to reprint the edition before the end of the year. This is especially true if the title contains a date, such as the *1997 Guide to the Far East*. The year on the front is like a big neon sign indicating an out-of-date book.

Try to get a feel for what the publisher is looking for before you write your query letter. Talk to an acquisitions editor, and do your library homework. If the publisher you are going to approach doesn't produce series, chances are it won't start one with you.

d. Recycle your research

Use the research you did for the book to write articles for newspapers and magazines. Most publishers will have no objection to you excerpting extensively from your own book, especially if it gives the book a plug. Many successful authors live off the same basic material for years.

e. Conduct informational seminars

Some writers successfully put on seminars to attract customers. Done correctly, these can be profitable, but they are time consuming and expensive to run. What if you put on a seminar and nobody comes?

Like anything else, seminars must be marketed to be successful. A common money-saving strategy is to focus on groups that have a means of alerting their members to your seminar. For instance, seniors' groups and volunteer organizations have newsletters in which you can announce your exclusive seminar, probably without cost. But look carefully at the types of prospects this may bring you. Rick once ran a seminar at an old-age home where he was assured everyone had a wonderful time drinking tea and listening to "that nice young man." It was virtually free to set up and run, but he didn't make one sale.

General advertising of your seminar, though more expensive, may give you more interested prospects. Advertising for seminars also seems to work much better than advertising for books.

Be sure to take advantage of any free public service announcements radio and TV stations may have. Small stations may be willing to do this for you; large stations probably won't. Also, check to see if any of your local community newspapers have a section called "What's On."

If you can, piggyback on the efforts of a tour operator that already gives seminars on the destination you've written about. It might allow you to sell your book at the back of the room.

Depending on the thrust of your book, you might be able to save on expenses by getting travel suppliers to kick in money or help. If you have a guidebook on Munich, for instance, the German tourist board may lend a hand with posters, personnel to answer questions, possibly a place to do the seminar, cash to defray rental expenses, and marketing. And don't forget to ask the destination's national airline, resorts, and hotel chains to participate.

Market your seminar aggressively. Make it the focus of your life for a month beforehand. Use advertising, tell existing book customers about it, and notify your contacts and acquaintances.

It is easy to do your own seminar, so do not pay to have someone put it on for you. If you rent their conference space, hotels will have suggestions, as well as hardware and audio visual equipment (although you will likely have to pay for the equipment).

These are some other points you may want to keep in mind:

(a) Check the calendar. Absolutely do not schedule your seminar during Christmas, Easter, spring break, major sporting events, or over a long weekend.

(b) Pick a central, easily accessible location.

(c) Keep it less than two hours in duration, plus a question and answer period.

(d) If you have an extraordinary guest speaker, you might charge admission, but most informational seminars are free.

(e) If you have written a destination-oriented book, try to convince local suppliers to give away free trips, T-shirts, and luggage in a draw. Stress this in all your marketing. It will dramatically increase attendance.

(f) Tickets and reservations work for and against you. They may make the seminar seem more valuable, but will also discourage last minute participants who think they must have a reservation to attend. Many of your prospects will decide at the last minute, and only 60% of people with reservations will show up.

(g) Have someone to help you with the sales of your book. After the seminar, you will be busy answering questions. You can't efficiently do sales and be the expert at the same time.

You will not want to give many talks without a clear indication that they work for you. Seminars require a lot of preparation and evening work. Make the first one count. If you push hard and it turns out the sales are low, you'll at least know your marketing effort was not the culprit.

f. Sell your book to travel agents

We know of at least two authors who make a living selling their books to travel agents. They visit travel agents who specialize in cruises and sell their book on cruise ship destinations. The agents, in turn, give the book to their clients as a "thank you" for purchasing a cruise. You won't make the 40% to 50% most retailers do on a book, but you can probably sell the book at or near the full price.

You might think marketing through travel agencies would be a another good marketing strategy. Their clients come in to arrange a trip and purchase your book at the same time. Unlikely. While we're sure a few books are sold to consumers this way, we have never heard of it being successful on a large scale.

The big obstacle is that the travel agency is then acting as a retail bookseller and wants the 40% any other bookseller would receive. This doesn't leave you much margin for profit. Even if you manage to reduce the travel agency's take to 35%, you still get only 5% to 15%. If they sell ten books at $14.95 each, you make only $22 or less. Hardly worth the effort.

g. Lectures

You can make money as a lecturer in several ways. You can hire yourself out to speak at luncheons as an expert or you can put together your own events. Holding lectures on your subject is a big money-maker for some established authors. As a new author, your chances of making money this way are slim, but watch for opportunities.

h. Sell a newsletter for updates

Cross-marketing books and newsletters can produce excellent results. Don't start a newsletter just to market your book, but if the newsletter idea stands on its own as a financially viable business, the book marketing is an added bonus.

For example, if you have a book on exploring Thai restaurants, you might mention in the book that readers can have monthly or quarterly updates on fabulous new restaurants in Thailand by subscribing to the newsletter *Hot Soup: The Travelers' Guide to the Spiciest Thai Restaurants*. Mentioning or favorably reviewing your own publications is a time-honored tradition among authors. The newsletter, of course, would have an order form to sell the book.

Another way to profit from your book is to offer it as a gift (called a premium) to new and renewing subscribers of your newsletter. Essentially, a portion of the price of the newsletter is earmarked to pay for the book. Like all other marketing tactics, the effectiveness of the premium must be evaluated. You want to be sure the cost of the book isn't more than other marketing options or incentives for your newsletter.

A big factor in favor of a newsletter is that it doesn't take much extra effort to market it at the same time as you market your book. You can use the same ordering and banking procedures for both (see section l. below on retailing your book), and you probably already have the equipment you need to produce the newsletter from writing the book. As well, all that research material that never got into the final version of your book can now be put to good use.

You can also discuss the newsletter and the book in the same interviews to maximize the returns on your media efforts.

If you are going this route, send for complimentary copies of as many newsletters as you can, both in and out of the travel field. With a minimum of research, you should be able to solve the selling price, size, format, and frequency of issues. Also have a look at the Self-Counsel Press book, *Producing a First-Class Newsletter*.

i. Run guided tours

Your book can give you a competitive edge if you also run tours to a destination featured in your book. After all, you are an acknowledged expert. Several authors do very well both in terms of money and lifestyle taking visitors to their favorite places.

Not everyone can pull this off. It takes a special kind of person to lead tours. But the rewards, free trips, and money make it worth having a look at this as an alternative way to cash in on your book. The Self-Counsel Press book, *Start and Run a Profitable Tour Guiding Business*, will tell you all you need to know about this exciting business.

j. Look for other writing projects

Look for other, more lucrative writing projects. The media will tout you as an expert even if you have only one book to your credit, and you will have a much easier time obtaining writing contracts for corporate brochures, guides, reviews, and newspaper columns than you did before you wrote that book. Don't forget to look around your hometown for private corporations or tourist attractions that might want to have a book written about them. These can be very lucrative.

As an example, one writer we know approached the organization operating a historical tourist attraction and asked if it was interested in a concise history of the attraction. The idea was enthusiastically received.

k. Teach

Depending on the book you write, you might be able to teach the contents in a night school or a one-day course at a local high school or university. The pay is not bad once you teach the course a couple of times. The first two or three times, you'll put in many hours setting up the course content. After that, you can relax into enjoying the teaching process.

Of course, guess whose book is the required text? Have plenty of copies with you.

l. Retail your book

Selling your book retail can range from an occasional sale to a fully fledged retail mail-order operation complete with toll-free ordering telephone lines.

A retail bookstore usually makes between 40% and 50% of the retail cover price. If you have a way to sell your book directly to the public, take advantage of it. Even a modest number of retail sales each year will add to your book's profitability.

Talk to your publisher to see what wholesale price you can arrange and what kind of volume you need. Also check to find out if it has any objection to your generating publicity and then directing potential customers to you, rather than the publisher. Here are some suggestions.

1. Install a toll-free telephone line

Toll-free telephone lines are cheap, and potential customers like the idea of not having to pay for a long-distance phone call to make a purchase. This is an ordering line only. If a person is calling for any other reason, have him or her call your regular long-distance number. You must guard against people who call to pick your brains or just have a chat with the author. The long-distance bills can really eat up your profits, so be polite but firm about getting that person off the phone unless he or she is ordering.

Answer the phone when you are home and have an answering machine pick up when you aren't. Have a message that tells the caller he or she has reached the order line for your book (name the title), and that no one can help now. Then tell how to buy a copy of your book (e.g., send a check or leave the credit card number).

2. About advertising

Every advertiser's dream is to run a little ad that generates a very good profit. You know, three little lines in the *National Enquirer*. Then, so the story goes, a few more ads in different places. All of them make a little cash. Eventually there are dozens of classified ads running across the continent bringing in thousands of dollars a month. There's even a late-night infomercial about how to become a millionaire just by running little ads.

Rubbish! In this fairy tale there is no glass slipper and instead of two shrew sisters and an evil stepmother, you'll have the accounts receivable departments of several magazines and newspapers hounding you to pay for all the ads you ordered.

Don't spend a penny on this type of advertising. First, most ads do not bring in big gains. If they did, publishers would have done this long ago. Publishers have spent large amounts of research money learning the greatest returns come from targeting bookstores and libraries, not the consumer.

Second, there are hidden costs. There is no point in running ads if no one is there to answer the phones for the orders coming in. You'd have to hire an answering service.

3. Publicity

Publicity (articles and interviews), as opposed to advertising, has more impact on potential readers than anything except possibly a word-of-mouth recommendation from a friend. If the reviewer says your book is a must-read or the interview keeps listeners tuned in, you've got an endorsement money can't buy. Best of all, it doesn't cost much and the retail book sales generated by the publicity can go a long way toward making a living for you.

Fortunately, the media thrives on the new and exotic, and your travel book might be just the ticket. It should be relatively easy to obtain at least a few interviews.

If your publisher did some initial publicity, don't be afraid to go back to these same stations and magazines six months later. Those that didn't do an interview initially may want one now. Others may want an update. A constant publicity campaign is one of the best ways to generate income.

Papers may be interested in destination articles written by you, especially if you've written a guidebook. If you feel comfortable in front of the camera or on the radio, push for an interview. Naturally you'll give the audience a taste of what your book is about and that all-important ordering information.

Publicity is very time consuming, but if you are willing to make the commitment to a concerted campaign, and if you have an imaginative approach to a topic, it can pay handsomely. Here's what you need to do to get an interview.

(a) Write a press release

Write a snappy headline and a very short paragraph about the topics you are interested in talking about. It must be new or exotic and cannot be just a commercial for your book.

The physical layout of a press release can vary, but some things are fairly standard. Put your name, address, phone number, and the date in the upper righthand corner of each page. Most press releases are one page, occasionally two, but never more. Short and punchy is the idea. Sample #12 is an example of a press release.

(b) Research stations, papers, or magazines

Research the TV and radio stations, papers, or magazines you are interested in. Select the most promising based on their audience and the format or topics they like to use, and mail them a copy of your news release.

Date your press release a few days after you expect to mail it so it keeps it as fresh looking as possible. Editors and announcers throw out anything they feel is so old that they will have to check all the information by phone to verify its validity. There are just too many competing stories for them to keep their work load under control otherwise.

Contact: Jennifer King
(600) 555-1412

Lifestyles or Travel Editor

Press Release

$99 FLIGHTS TO HONG KONG??!!

Yes, $99 round trip from North America! Our newsletter, *Travel on a Dime,* has information on courier flights (that's how a passenger flew to Hong Kong for $99), delivery flights for aircraft, scams that defraud travelers, bucket shops, last minute sell-offs, stand-by air-fares, coupon trading and much more.

The subscription is $39 per year.
A sample issue of *Travel on a Dime* is enclosed.
Please feel free to use any of the enclosed articles.

Contact: Jennifer King
Phone: (600) 555-1412
             1234 Meltdown Place
             Beggarsville, CA

Some writers like to establish a relationship with editors and producers and personally address press releases to start on the right foot. If this is your preferred style, call each one to find the name of the person who produces a news show or is in charge of travel news. Keep this information in a database and learn how to use the mail merge function of your word processor.

As an alternative, one that takes less time but costs a bit more money per interview, skip a lot of the research and data entry and just address your press release to "the editor," or "the news producer." This is a lot less effort, you avoid insulting the current editor by addressing your correspondence to the previous editor or by calling him or her Editor in Chief instead of Chief Editor (true story, and it was a nasty little reply note, too), and your press release doesn't languish unopened because it was personally addressed to a producer or editor who is no longer there.

Having tried both ways, we favor less work. Even though on a per letter basis, the personal approach works better than non-personalized letters, we still prefer to send out a larger, non-personalized shot gun publicity blast, hoping the story will snag the interview on its own merits. We tend not to be too fussy about what kind of programs or papers we send it to. We've had some pleasant surprises from which media outlets have taken an interest.

The point of publicity is to put your phone number for ordering your book before the public. There is no secondary objective.

(c) Follow up

Follow up a personalized mailing about a week later with a phone call. Make sure your release was received and ask if that contact would be interested in talking to you further. At this point, you will either receive an invitation or a refusal.

With a non-personalized press release program, skip the expensive long-distance follow-up phone calls and spend the money you save on another mailing a few weeks later.

Go back to the same source three to six months later and tell him or her about the update you can do. Stations that receive dozens of calls after your interview will want you back.

(d) Sweet talk editors and producers

Interviews and appearances boost your credibility and fill out your bio as a well-rounded travel expert. So even if your book is only a small part of a show sandwiched in between other topics and doesn't bring you big sales, you still win. Just be aware that once you have done a few dozen interviews, the benefit to your bio or as a training exercise decreases. At some point the only real reason to prepare and do interviews is for book sales.

The only caveat with all publicity is it must be done right. If you are retailing your book, people must be able to contact you. From sad experience we can tell you an interview in any media, no matter how many readers or viewers hear your message, is wasted unless you can get your telephone number on the air.

A forthright approach is best. When Barbara and Rick first started, they did a lot of work for interviewers helping to prepare them for the interview. They took on time-consuming tasks such as preparing a list of questions for them to ask, looking up statistics they had expressed interest in, even finding other guests who might go on the show. After all the extra work, when Rick and Barbara shyly asked if the interviewers would put their phone number in the interview, several hosts refused. Rick and Barbara did the interviews and regretted the effort. The lesson here is to ask up-front about your telephone number. Make it clear you are not interested in the interview if your number is not also broadcast.

After several stations refused to give out Barbara and Rick's telephone number, because it appeared too commercial and was not news, Barbara and Rick came up with the idea of a free mail-out for their audience. They wrote one page of information for each specific hook they used on the air. They had handouts on tours and destinations, consumer pieces on senior citizens' discounts, travel contests, and health and safety while traveling. All the listener or viewer had to do was call the number to receive the blurb free of charge.

This always worked. Radio and TV love the idea of their audience receiving something for free, and Rick and Barbara got to build their mailing list! Of course, they enclosed an advertisement about their book with every request, and this generated sales.

To carry these ideas a little further, try working your way into a regular newscast. Offer to appear on a weekly basis to tell the audience about the best deals of the week or comment on changes in the travel industry. Of course, in return for all this hard work, you expect the station to mention your book and phone number, or to pay you, or both. Ideally, you offer extra information too, and you can try to cash in a second time by mailing your advertisement with the information mail-out.

This strategy will require a long-term campaign of press releases and articles aimed at the media outlets you are pursuing. The more the show's producer sees your work or hears you in interviews, the more likely he or she is to call you as a travel expert when something noteworthy happens in the field of travel. If you let it be known you would like to do more, you'll be at the top of the list.

As you might guess, TV interviews generate the most response while radio programs aired at the drive to or from work and interviews for major newspapers and magazines run a close second. Interviews for small magazines and papers are not terrific sales generators, but they do not take much time either. (Many are done over the phone.)

12

The downside of the writing business

or How to re-wallpaper your bathroom
for the cost of a postage stamp
(or two, or three...)

There's no question about it. Travel writing is exciting, fun, educational, rewarding, and a whole lot more.

So why isn't every globe-trotter taking up pen and paper? Because, like any other business, there is a downside lurking behind the glamour and prestige. This chapter is about surviving the dog days (and late nights) of travel writing.

a. Don't let rejection stop you

Taped to Susan's computer is a pearl of wisdom she passes on to all her students. She's never been able to discover the author, but the advice is priceless.

> *Be patient. Be polite. Be persistent. IT PAYS! 48% give*
> *up after the first rejection. About 10% resubmit over*
> *four times. 80% of sales are made after the fifth try.*

Rejection is part of the business of writing. Never forget it's your successes, not your rejections, that are important. When you get a rejection slip, remember that it didn't appear out of thin air. You had to do something worthwhile to get it — you wrote and submitted an article or an idea to an editor. Maybe the first editor didn't like it, or the second, or the third. But somewhere down the line an editor somewhere *will* like what you're proposing. As long as you're willing to continue sending your words out into the marketplace.

And remember, persistence does pay off. Submitting pieces to the same people over and over again is like Chinese water torture. Eventually, for relief, they may publish one of your stories.

And in the meantime, rejection slips make a unique and inexpensive wallpaper that's guaranteed to be a conversation piece. Display them with pride.

b. Get up faster than you fall

Even the most established travel writer sends out proposals that are returned with a polite, if impersonal, "Thanks, but no thanks" cover letter. These are the moments when it's vital to remember that timing is as important as writing ability. It won't matter how scintillating your prose, a marketplace saturated with stories about Ireland isn't going to buy your firsthand experience about rainbows and leprechauns. Look for a new and unique angle if you want to pursue marketing your tale of the Orange and the Green.

c. Don't take form rejection letters personally

It often seems like a slap in the face when an impersonal form letter is the only response after all the blood, sweat, and tears of writing an article. The reality is editors, especially ones who work at large publications, simply don't have the time to write a personalized note. Some don't even bother to send a form letter; we've all received more than one query or submission back with nothing more than a few words scrawled across the top. A few had no indication whether or not it had even been read, they just showed up in the mail box.

When this happens to you, and it will, remember that editors are notoriously overworked professionals. It's nothing personal, they just don't have time to write notes to the 20, 30, or 50 people each day who submit.

d. Learn from rejection

Sometimes an editor may give you an indication of the main reason your idea wasn't suitable for the particular market you targeted. This

As soon as you've written a query or an article, make a list of potential markets. Start with the one that pays the most and submit there first. If that publisher isn't interested, send it out to the next one on your list — the same day you receive the rejection slip!

If you reach the end, start again from the beginning. It's surprising how often editorial requirements change as editors move from one publication to another. We've actually submitted the same idea to the same editor 18 months later and ended up with a sale the second time round.

can be anything from a tick-off-the-box form to a quick note scrawled in the margin of your query. If your idea was very close to the mark, you may even get a short, personal note from the editor. Any of these are cause to celebrate and learn. After all, the more you know about why *ABC Travel Magazine* didn't accept your article on the Grand Canyon, the more you can tailor your newest idea about the Moors of Scotland to its requirements.

e. Health hazards

Believe it or not, a writing career has some health risks. Carpal tunnel syndrome, neck problems, tingling hands, and tendonitis are just a few of the painful and debilitating problems that can visit you. An inability to sleep comes with the pain, and tired cranky writers are not productive writers.

Before experiencing any symptoms — tender wrists, shooting pain radiating from your elbow, and muscle cramps — you should take a few precautions. Once these symptoms start, they are difficult to cure, and especially in this business, have a big tendency to get worse.

Use the following tips to practice preventive maintenance for body and spirit.

(a) Stretch every hour. Stand up when you do — it forces you to move away from your computer or desk. Inhale and exhale deeply, and really allow your body to relax.

(b) At least three or four times a day, look out a window or step outside your door. Hold your hand approximately six inches in front of your face. Focus on your hand for three seconds. Now switch your focus to something that's as far away as possible — a tree on the horizon or the mountains or even a neighbor's house. Switch back and forth several times to exercise your eye muscles.

(c) Your typewriter or keyboard should be level with your arms when they are bent 90 degrees from your body.

(d) To prevent neck problems, sit as straight as you can. This takes a bit of practice if you are prone to slouching, but it puts the least strain on your joints and muscles and increases your endurance. Check into the various back supports that attach to most office chairs if you have trouble with this.

(e) Your chair should be adjustable. At the very least you need to be able to change the height; it's better if you can adjust the back rest and slope of the seat as well. Since you will spend many hours with this tool, spend some money on a good one. Even if you can only afford secondhand, buy the very best you can.

(f) Many writers say propping their feet up six inches or so off the floor is helpful. There are foot rests available for this, but at $35 and up, we prefer an old box or stack of magazines.

(g) Always have adequate lighting. If you get headaches frequently when working and you know you haven't been pounding your noggin in frustration, try a different light source or move the one you have.

(h) Don't sit in a draft. Susan once found her back muscles going into spasm for no apparent reason. Eventually, she discovered that by moving her desk three feet to the right several days earlier, she had placed herself directly in front of the blast of cold air from an air conditioning unit. A simple return to her original spot, and she was back in business and in comfort.

(i) Take a break to pamper yourself. Whatever you do, take your body's warnings seriously. Don't give in to the old aspirin-will-make-the-pain-go-away routine. Masking pain now is a great way to cripple your production later, and most writers don't have long-term disability insurance.

There will be times when all you want to do is throw your hands in the air and give up. The most important and worthwhile thing you can do for yourself on those days is to take a break. Do something you love—play tennis, walk along a beach with your dog, have a bubblebath by candlelight, go for lunch with your best friend, pick wildflowers in the forest.

As long as you have other things in your life, you'll most often find you are able to come back to your writing feeling refreshed, inspired, and able to laugh at the inevitable rejection slips. Besides, what other profession allows you to wallpaper your bathroom for the cost of a postage stamp?

13

Looking good

We used to daydream that every editor we submitted a manuscript to admired (all right, was absolutely stunned by) the perfection of our prose, the obvious commercial appeal of our work, and was scrambling to find a pen to sign a check for us. We would probably have been better off daydreaming about wearing a red cape and blue tights while we hand delivered the manuscript through the tenth-floor window.

We all want to make a good impression on editors and sponsors. Even the best, most established writer needs to pay constant attention to packaging himself or herself to make a good impression. If your manuscript arrives looking like writer's road kill, an editor may pass on tasting the meat of your work in favor of some pristine morsel from the slush pile. Illegible letters and scrawled faxes without identifying information send a clear message that you don't really care. Sponsors or editors have too many other would-be authors with neat, concise proposals awaiting their attention to spend time deciphering a handwritten proposal.

To give yourself every edge you can, you need to project a competent image and the right impression. Here's how to do it.

a. Telephone communication

It has been said elsewhere, but bears repeating. If you are going to use your home line and other people answer the phone, make sure they can all answer the phone in a business-like manner and write a coherent, accurate message. We've had the pleasure of hearing young children do a pretty good rendition of the efficient secretary, so we know they can be trained.

It is important you and the caller can rely on the message-taker to convey the facts to you correctly. If you don't think there is any way in the world the other members of your household can take down a message of more than four words, put in a separate line that only you answer.

Answering machines should give the caller a crisp, clean, and short message. Check your machine once a month to be sure the sound quality is still good. Change your tape or message when it needs refreshing.

b. Letters, letterhead, and other paper stuff

Often, you'll be able to sit at home in your tatty bathrobe and deal with people over the phone, by fax, or by mail. Your bad-hair day won't sink you, but poorly presented paperwork could. Remember, you are presenting yourself as someone who has a way with words.

Proofread and edit carefully, and use the spell-checking program on your computer. Susan has a sign over her computer which reads, "It never hurts to spell check one more time." This little reminder has saved her more times than she cares to count.

For the sake of efficiency, keep your business letters as short as possible. The less there is, the less there is to gum up the message. Short declarative sentences using active voice and strong verbs are best.

1. Stationery

It is also worth your time to put effort into the stationery you choose to put forth to the world. You'll need letterhead, fax cover sheets, envelopes, and business cards. A 20 lb bond paper is economical and looks good. You don't have to go the route of embossing, color, and heavy weight stock. Neat and clean is all you really need.

If you have computer software with layout capabilities and a laser printer, there is no reason why you can't create your own business design on good quality paper. Simple designs are best. Look at what other people have done to generate your own ideas. All that is really required is your identifying information (name, address, phone number, plus fax and e-mail numbers if you have them) somewhere prominently on the page.

If you are using a typewriter or a basic computer and printer without a selection of print choices (fonts), your options will be more limited. But even with a dot matrix printer you can still set up basic stationery for yourself. Alternatively, you can go to a print shop and purchase a coordinated stationery package of envelopes, business cards, and letterhead. If you shop carefully and stick with black type on white paper, you should be able to find all you need for under $100.

2. Business cards

Business cards are a necessity. Not only do they give all the information about who you are and what you do in an easily stored format, but more important, they convey the message that you are serious about what you do.

You should hand them out frequently, and always have a supply on hand. Include one with everything you mail out, and have a lot on hand when you visit any travel trade shows.

Try to keep your business card straightforward. Publishing is still a somewhat genteel industry, and fancy titles serve only to mark you as brash or harebrained. You may be the chief executive officer of your writing company, but everyone will eventually know you are also the company's chief gofer too.

Some creative souls do come up with catchy titles that work. "Rhonda the Writer" is to the point. When in doubt, before you immortalize your title on paper, ask a few business friends if the title you have chosen for yourself is too playful or too grand.

Writers with multiple jobs will make it easier for everyone else if they list their various titles. For instance, if you are a columnist and a freelance writer, put both on your card. Barbara once had cards that didn't tell the whole story, and she always ending up explaining far more than she wanted to, or writing little notes on her card before giving them away. Eventually she had new cards printed and life became much simpler.

If you write for a publication on a regular basis, put the newspaper or magazine's name on your business card, not the name of the company publishing the paper. The publisher may not be a name anyone recognizes, while many people will know the name of the publication. Be sure you check with the management about their policy regarding business cards first. Regular freelance contributors may have to specify freelance to distinguish themselves from staff writers.

Some people prefer to leave the word "freelance" off their business card. They feel the sponsors may feel they can't really rely on

Having an e-mail address is rapidly becoming something expected of a professional in any area of writing. Even though it is still considered impolite to e-mail an editor without his or her specific invitation to do so, be sure to include your e-mail address on your business card and letterhead.

Team writers can avoid confusion by making one card for both people. It also eliminates dealing with duplicates of every press or news release issued.

having a particular project published because there is no affiliation with a guaranteed outlet. "Writer" leaves it more open. We use both expressions, depending on the circumstances, and haven't noticed a problem with either.

3. Fax machines and computer communications

Fax machines are indispensable for the travel writer and are another opportunity to look good to the outside world. Every fax going out of your office should carry a typed cover sheet with your name, your company's name if you have one, your address, phone, and fax numbers, and some advertising for your business.

c. Your bio

If you want to make a positive impression with an editor (or with a supplier when requesting a trip), you must let him or her know you can produce great work. The customary way is to send a biography along with your query letter.

Your biography is simply a résumé of your published work — a list of everything you have to your writing credit — along with some other pertinent details about yourself. Especially if you are not the world's most gifted schmoozer, your bio will say for you what you would be too embarrassed to mumble out in a cold call to an editor: you are professional, finish your work by deadline, won't demand too much time, and you know your stuff. Otherwise, why would all these people publish you?

Your bio also gives you credibility as a travel expert. It should succinctly show your experience. You can use that experience to influence someone to give you a trip, listen to your proposal, read your work, give you an interview, even lend you equipment.

You will probably have anywhere from two to a dozen different bios with information or layouts tailored for various situations. You might have one that lists all your quotes, interviews, and published articles, with details about the theme of the articles and their publication dates. Another might list broadcast experience only. Yet another might simply list the magazine name and the date your article appeared.

1. What should be on your bio

Everyone has a different idea of what should be included in a bio. Some purists insist travel articles or books published are the only

Winfax Pro by Delrina, as well as several other computer fax programs, has nifty fax cover pages for almost every occasion. They are worth checking out — at least for ideas — and many of them can be modified to give you a snazzy look without paying for the services of a commercial illustrator.

legitimate items. Others writers also include TV or radio interviews about travel that feature them as the main guest.

The ideal bio establishes you as an expert in the field of travel. A long list of articles published and wide variety of titles show a wide knowledge. Your bio displays the fact that other people value your opinion. After all, they have published, quoted, or excerpted your work.

In addition to a list of your published works, you may want to list business experience or education relating to your travel writing. Anything that displays your flexibility, knowledge, and ability to promote yourself is useful in a bio. If you were quoted extensively as an expert, or interviewed for your opinion, or even had a letter to the editor published, you can use this to show your recognized expertise.

The bio shown in Sample #13 is a short overview of the writer's experience, mentioning travel books written, major radio and TV appearances, some selected magazine and newspaper articles, business experience, and education. Individual articles are not highlighted.

We usually use an overview bio, but will send out the more extensive one when we want less emphasis on our business experience or education and more on what we've had published. Sample #14 is an example of an extended bio.

d. Keeping track

1. Print media

It takes effort, but it's essential to collect and keep copies of all the published articles and tapes of interviews you do. At some point someone will want to see something you've listed on your bio.

If an article showcases your work in a particularly favorable way, you may want to use it as a promo piece for yourself. We always have copies of two or three favorite articles stuck in the file with our bio so they are handy if someone asks for an example of our work.

As a matter of routine, you should think about how you are going to acquire copies of any articles or radio, print, or TV interviews that quote you. Don't sit back expecting copies to arrive on your doorstep. It almost never happens. You need to have a plan to obtain them, and follow through relentlessly.

Articles in major national magazines or local papers are easy. Go to the store and buy a copy (or 20, for the relatives). However, obtaining a copy of a newspaper in a far off place can be agony. If you have friends there, ask them to pick up a copy as soon as it comes

MARY JAMESON

Newspaper columnist

Mary writes a weekly freelance column for the travel section of the *Times,* a major daily newspaper in Anytown.

Books published

Her first book, *Travel the World on the Cheap,* was published in 1996 and is now in its fourth printing. Her second book on travel is scheduled for publication in the spring of 1998.

Magazine articles

Mary has contributed travel and consumer information articles to many magazines on a freelance basis.

Television and radio

Mary has been invited to appear on dozens of radio and television shows across Canada and the U.S. Interviews include national broadcasts on ZBC Television's *That's Life Today* and *Travel the World.*

Teaching

Mary has been teaching travel writing courses at the college level for the last four years.

Newsletter

As well, Mary edits and publishes a national consumer travel newsletter, *Travel on a Dime,* which reports on destinations and travel bargains.

Education

Mary has a degree from McGoo University in Major Town.

Photocopies of articles are available on request.

1537 Your Street, Anytown Phone: (600) 555-7654 Fax: (600) 555-7653

Articles Published by Mary Jameson

"Don't Travel without Reading these Tips," *Money Saving*, April 1997

"Windsurf the Columbia Gorge," *Windy Life*, March 1997

"Living Over the Water In Tahiti," *Postcards From Heaven*, December 1996

Interviews

"Let's Go," XROZ, Majortown TV interview, February 1997

"Travel the World," XCX, nationwide call-in radio show, January 1997

"That's Life Today," ZBZ, nationwide TV interview, November 1996

"Move it," XJOX, Anytown, radio talk show interview, November 1996

Reviews of Jameson's Publications

"Travel the World on the Cheap," reviewed in "Shirley's Corner" column, *West Coast Life*, October 1996

"Travel on a Dime," reviewed in "Books to Have" column, *DenverHerald*, Fall 1996

"Travel the World on the Cheap," reviewed in "Keep your Money" column, *Montreal Post*, August 1996

Quotes from Jameson's Publications

"Travel the World on the Cheap," quoted in "Mike Chats" column, *This World*, August 1996

"Travel the World on the Cheap," quoted in "Bits and Pieces" column, *LA Globe*, October 1996

"Travel on a Dime," quoted in "Sources to Check" column, *CheapTravel*, January 1996 out and mail it to you. Or call a contact in any organization, travel-related or not, that you belong to. Alumni associations are often great for this.

Some editors will help, but they are usually so busy they simply don't have the time to make it a high priority. Some papers do send articles out as a matter of course, but more often than not you will need to call the circulation desk and pay for a copy to be sent to you. These costs add up when you factor in the long-distance telephone call, the paper, and the postage. It is easy to spend $10 for just one copy.

Magazine articles are usually easier to acquire by directly contacting the editor who worked on your story. The editor is also more likely to automatically send you several copies of the issue you appeared in.

It happened to each one of us. When our first published article appeared, we bought more than one copy (but less than 100). But we learnt that after the first few times our relatives had seen us in print, we could safely reduce our cost by purchasing only one or two copies for our files. We quickly found it was expensive to ship a whole magazine. And, as we discovered, most people wanted just a photocopy of the article. We have never been asked to ship the entire publication to an editor.

2. Radio and TV interviews

You will need to plan ahead if you want a copy of you doing a TV interview. TV stations usually make copies by transferring from broadcast quality tape to VHS, often with a lot of growling from the librarian who has to find the tape and then from an editor who has to transfer it. TV stations rarely want anything to do with producing copies, regardless of the station's size.

If you are on a local station, your best bet is to tape the show yourself; if it's out of town, impose on friends and relatives to do it for you. Find out exactly when the interview will air, and remind your camera person on that day. Obtaining copies from any source a few days after an event is next to impossible.

Radio stations are generally more agreeable about helping out with requests for copies providing you let them know before the broadcast. After the broadcast, someone has to find the tape of the program and make a copy for you. You are, after all, asking them to do a favor for you, so show as much courtesy as you can and you'll get much better results.

No matter what you do, you won't have copies of all your broad-casts. Get what you can and don't worry about the rest.

3. Organizing your articles and tapes

Some writers prefer to keep their article copies in numbered files with ready-to-go copies in a folder behind the original. If you have the space to do this, it can save time, especially if you need to run down to the local photocopy outlet to make copies.

Some writers throw copies in a box where it is in more or less chronological order. When someone wants a particular article, they dig down and make a copy of it.

You may also want to consider cross-referencing your list of published clips in a computerized data base. Just remember that the real purpose is to have your copies easily available. Ultimately, whatever method works best for you is the one to use, but be meticulous about immediately adding a notation to your bio. It should always be up-to-date and ready to go. An updated bio also means you have an informal index.

14

Your name in lights

a. You as a travel expert

As you write your articles and books, prepare yourself for your television debut. If you write travel long enough, you will eventually be asked to give a lecture, do a television interview, appear on an open-line talk show, or be interviewed about one of your subjects for a major paper or magazine.

Not only is it fun, but interviews are career enhancing. The energy and time you spend on preparing for your 15 minutes of fame will lead directly to more money, better trips, and easier assignments. When you add the interview to your bio, it increases your credibility with sponsors. You obviously have a channel to the viewers or listeners they want to reach. You are a travel expert.

A lot of cross-pollination goes on in media. An interesting article lends itself to a captivating radio interview. Terrific pictures can do wonders for a limp travel piece on TV. Writing a book makes you enough of an expert that many newspapers will at least consider your application to do a column.

If you want a career in radio or TV, doing a TV interview will give you an "in": you won't have to do what thousands of hopefuls do and send in an application blind. Your interviews will put you in contact with the right people, and these people will have a chance to see you on air. If you want to lecture about travel, mentioning a couple of TV appearances on your lecture advertisements will fetch a bigger audience.

For all of these reasons, you should spend time each week looking at other media outlets for your travel writing. It makes you a more well-rounded travel writer, and it certainly gives you more options and alternatives.

b. Promoting yourself

You absolutely, positively must learn the crass art of self-promotion to get interviews. There are listeners who want to hear what you have to say, but unless a talk show host or producer learns about you and your subject, your message, regardless of how important or entertaining, will not reach anyone.

The idea that someone will discover you once you have a few articles published is a dream similar to winning the lottery. Before we caught on to how the publicity game worked, we were never invited for interviews. It wasn't the material we wrote. We used the same material for interviews we had been writing about for years. The difference was the media campaign we launched. To reap the benefits, you must have a plan.

First, come up with several provocative or informative topics. The easiest way to tell if the topics are suitable is to imagine you are the host of the talk show and you are telling listeners what's up next on the show: "And after the news, travel writer Kristin Cross will tell us how to keep our children safe while traveling overseas." Radio talk show hosts have a well-tuned ear for what listeners want. Would your listeners keep the dial where it is?

Radio announcer: "Where do you think is the most dangerous vacation spot in North America? What port would you guess the U.S. Navy stopped calling at because they had so many sailors hurt or killed there? No, it's not Los Angeles or New York."

Radio announcer: "My next guest can tell you how to fly to South America round trip for $70 or to Hong Kong for $60. You fly with big-name airlines, have your movies, meals, and even your frequent flyer miles. Want to know how? Stay tuned after the break."

This role-playing technique works because it takes you out of your usual critical self and lets your subconscious take over. You've heard a million programs. Somewhere in the back of your brain, you know what's interesting. By play acting a radio host, you can get a pretty valid opinion as to what will rivet an audience's (or radio host's) attention.

Consumer information about saving money traveling or staying healthy and safe are always hits.

Once you have a theme, boil it down to a phrase or, at most, a sentence. This is the lead for your press release. The shorter the better. We are inundated with mail and press releases every day. We do not have time to read them all. If the opening sentence is badly constructed or uninteresting, we throw it out. All the editors and talk show producers we know are under the same avalanche.

Next, in a paragraph, two at the most, state a little more about your topic. Again keep it brief. Extra verbiage impedes the message and is a good excuse for the reader to put the press release aside or throw it out. Don't try to tell the whole story here. We usually include background material in the form of an article we've written on a separate page. (Note the placement of the phone number and name in Sample #12 in chapter 11.)

c. Your contact list

For an initial mailing list, think of all the radio and TV talk shows you listen to. Whose column do you read? Once you write a list, call each station and confirm its address and the correct spelling of the host or writer's name.

We add to our mailing lists all the time. We have a box we throw ideas into, and once a month or so, we sit down and find addresses and enter them in the computer. We also swap lists with other writers who understand this process and create lists too.

Occasionally, we buy a list, but we have never found this satisfactory. Generally, the list is not specialized enough, and we spend days wading through thousands of addresses to pull out the few dozen we might use. Sometimes the lists are too specialized, for example, giving TV or radio stations in Arizona only.

To do this job efficiently, you will need to learn to use a computerized database. There is no sense in handwriting each address every time you wish to use it. By entering the data into the computer once, you can use it forever.

Any computer can handle a database, so you do not need top-of-the-line equipment. For a printer, use one of those old obsolete nine-pin printers ($30 secondhand). The easiest and cheapest labels to use are continuous feed, single up labels. You don't need to purchase expensive laser printer labels, though they do give you a cleaner, professional looking print out for a penny a label or less.

Put the lead in large, easy-to-read, bold letters, and one short paragraph in normal 12-point sized print on one page of your press release. All other background material should be in the package, but on other pages.

Don't reuse a dated press release from a month ago to save on printing costs. It is false economy. Editors and announcers throw out anything they feel is so old that they will have to check all the information by phone to verify its validity.

Travel trade shows are a great place to get on many media lists in just a couple hours, rather than writing individual request letters and faxes. Make sure you pass out your business cards liberally.

Hire a computer nerd to set it all up, unless you love fiddling with computers. And don't pay $50 an hour. There are starving students who will do it for you inexpensively. Call the computer department of your local university or the secretarial training school. They will probably know someone who needs part-time work. All those kids who used to type term papers now do data entry and know databases, so you shouldn't have trouble finding inexpensive help.

Public relations firms specialize in putting your name before the public and they generally do a good job. But they are also expensive. If you've got the money but not the time, hire a public relations firm to organize a mailing list and do your press releases and mailing.

d. Preparing for the interview

Print interviews are easy. The reporter asks a bunch of questions, and you answer them. If you don't know, tell the reporter you will find out. The interview may be spread out over several days, as you find a relevant background article for the reporter to read, or answer new questions as they come up. Generally, print interviews are more in-depth than those on radio or TV. There is time to do background research and writing articles is a slower-paced process than the electronic media.

You'll quickly find print interviews are just another conversation. You still need to organize what you want to say beforehand, but it is less crucial you cover everything the first time.

With radio and TV, you can't stop the interview to look for more information or think about the answer to a question. It may help you to make an outline ahead of time, much as you would when writing an article, but things will always come out of left field in a live interview.

Here's some useful advice to make the most of the interview:

(a) Memorize a few points you want to make so the listener will understand the subject easily. Write these up in point form, just short, quick reminder phrases. Practice them until you don't leave anything out. Don't make up an entire script of everything you want to say. Unless you are a consummate actor, you'll come off sounding wooden.

(b) Think about the questions you will likely be asked and come up with a well-rehearsed answer.

You don't think talk show hosts read all the books they interview authors about, do you? Sometimes you will need to save an unprepared interviewer from themselves. We have had some really off-the-wall questions because the interviewer thought we were someone else. "So, were the hydroelectric projects in India comparable to ours here?" Uh, oh!

As a precaution, talk with the host before the segment to make sure he or she knows what the interview is about. We usually try to speak with the host the day before and feed him or her questions to ask. Some see this as a real time saver and are very receptive, while a few want to wing it on air.

(c) Act naturally, well, as naturally as you can with bright lights in your eyes and someone breaking in to go to commercials every few minutes.

(d) Learn to be long-winded. Simple yes or no answers to questions make the interviewer work too hard to keep the conversation going, and everyone else falls asleep. People love to hear stories, so spice your remarks liberally with anecdotes to illustrate your point. Listeners also like statistics in small doses. Unless you are a professional comedian, never tell jokes.

(e) Watch other shows and see how many times the guests change the tone or the direction of the interview with their answers. This requires a little practice, but it is an essential tool.

Such a skill is useful if the host asks questions you don't know the answer to or that are completely off topic. Just keep returning to the message you want to put across.

(f) Try this trick if you need time to think about something: "John, before we get to that, I wanted to tell you about...," and then launch into something you've held in reserve. You can also delay by asking the host to repeat the question if it is particularly complicated. Don't use this with simple questions: "So you wrote this article about diseases and children traveling?" "Could you repeat that, Dave?"

(g) Let the interviewer know during the break if something is wrong with the equipment. Phone interviews are susceptible to static, and ear pieces do fall out.

(h) Keep any glasses of water well away from you during the interview, especially if you are prone to talking with your hands. If you upset it while making a point, you'll say things not on the FCC and CRTC list of approved broadcast phrases.

(i) Smile. Whether you are on TV or radio. It will come through in your voice.

(j) Be careful not to hum, tap your feet, pat the microphone, or ask yourself out loud what you are doing here. Never, ever, say anything during a commercial break that you don't want to go out over the air. The microphone is open more often than you think.

Remember, interviewers want you to succeed. We've gone blank on the air, inadvertently given out our home instead of office telephone number, and spoken in an entirely indecipherable language. Each time the interviewer calmly saved us with a long comment or a gentle correction while we pulled it together again. It's their show and their job on the line, so they want to make it sound as professional as possible.

Generally, travel is not a confrontational subject. You'll not be ambushed by a reporter. This isn't investigative reporting where they are trying to catch you in an error.

e. Stage fright

Most of us suffer from severe stage fright before radio and TV interviews. It is natural to be excited or nervous, but some of us, including well-known actors and politicians, generate enough nervous energy to power a small town. Despite the unpleasant side effects, you likely still look forward to the experience. It's a thrill.

It does get better the more interviews you do. The first 30 seconds are the worst. After that, most people relax a bit as they become preoccupied with talking and answering questions.

Here are some suggestions for making stage fright easier on you.

(a) Take every opportunity you can to put yourself in that threatening place. Every time you succeed, you get stronger.

(b) Join Toastmasters. This organization, to help people with public speaking, is a wonderfully safe environment to get your feet wet. Even a few weeks can do wonders for your self-confidence and will give you a lot of practice dealing with your stage fright. If you faint, no one will care. At most meetings they'll just prop you back in your chair.

(c) Hum for several minutes before going on air to loosen your voice.

(d) Drink warm water if you need to drink water during the interview. Warm water is better than cold water for relaxing your vocal chords.

(e) Remember to breathe. And do it slowly.

(f) Your body sometimes betrays you. Your heart beats so rapidly that you become nervous because of the physical side effects. Talk to your physician. There are medications which are great for calming the physical nervous effects without killing your personality. It's important not to let all your energy disappear; you'll come across as lifeless.

(g) Stay away from alcohol or tranquilizers before an interview. You need your wits about you.

f. Pay me!

Unless you appear on a radio or TV show regularly, you are not likely to be compensated. But once you have appeared a few times as an expert on travel, you should inquire if there is any money to cover your research expenses.

Larger outfits, national broadcasters, or magazines may eventually offer payment if they use you regularly. Smaller companies usually won't, but it is still worth asking. Although regular paid columns and appearances on TV and radio are coveted and rare positions, they do open up.

Getting one of these positions is a lot like selling a book or magazine. Rather than applying through normal channels, find out which editor or producer is responsible for that particular position. Introduce yourself, and say you are interested in writing the column or appearing on air regularly.

Pitch the editor or producer on an idea. It should have all the elements of a press release: a strong idea with a catchy phrase that encapsulates the theme. Make sure he or she receives a business card and a bio so he or she knows who you are and what you can do. It helps immensely if you can send something regularly, for example, story ideas you think would be perfect for the show, that, of course, you just happen to have written about.

15
I'd like to procrastinate, but not today

"I've never been anywhere exciting. How can I be a travel writer?"

"I can only write when the muse strikes me."

"I'd love to write about my travels, but I don't have the time."

"I've always wanted to be a travel writer, and that's exactly what I'm going to be just as soon as _____." Possibilities to fill in the blanks for this one include:

- I retire
- my spouse retires
- I get a good job
- I have my own space and my own computer
- I've redecorated my office
- I've gone on my dream trip around the world
- my kids are in school
- my kids are in university
- my kids leave home
- I've finished the laundry and painted the house
- my dog learns how to play the violin

There are hundreds of reasons why people who say they want to write don't. Most of these stalling techniques are nothing more than procrastination or fear in one disguise or another — fear of failure, fear of success, fear of the possibility of success. It takes real courage to sit down, pen in hand, or, if you're like the majority of writers today, in front of a keyboard, and just write.

There are probably hundreds of books on the market offering solutions to time-management problems. Here are some of the ways we've found help us manage our writing time better. If your level of procrastination is more serious than these, buy a book or take some courses to help you.

a. Set realistic goals

Some professional writers assign themselves a certain number of hours each day during which they write; no phone calls, no laundry, no excuses. Others use total word count for the day as their measuring tape and may weed a bed of flowers or cook a batch of strawberry jam between the first and last word of the day.

We favor the words-per-day method because it makes it easier to plan. And the really good news is that the numbers don't have to be so large they become terrifying. If you faithfully wrote only 500 words per day, Monday to Friday, you'd be pumping out somewhere between 10 and 15 average-length articles per month. In nine months, you'd have 90,000 words, or the first draft of a good-length travel book. And if you increased your commitment to seven days a week, that first draft would be ready in just over half a year.

It doesn't really matter whether you choose one of these methods or another one altogether, a tiny step every day will eventually bring you to your goal. The important thing is to set goals you can live with but that will still lead you to the final destination of publication.

And on those rare days when you simply don't get a lot written, give yourself permission to forego the guilt trip. It will only make it harder to get back into writing the next day. As long as you remain aware of the difference between procrastinating and accepting that there will, on occasion, be unexpected interruptions you can't avoid, you'll soon be producing more words with less trauma than you ever imagined.

b. Identify your personal top ten list of time wasters

Identify your personal top ten list of time wasters. Here are some of ours:

(a) Phone calls

(b) Having a "quick" cup of tea and a muffin

(c) Phone calls

(d) Lusting after computer gadgets and gizmos

(e) Unnecessary paper handling and filing

(f) Phone calls

(g) Sorting the in-basket for the tenth time

(h) Reviewing notes/research for the twentieth time

(i) Returning phone calls

The one great thing about procrastination is that it's self-correcting. Miss a few deadlines, and you won't have any projects to procrastinate about. Published authors are not procrastinators.

Once we realized the phone was the single biggest time waster, we began setting aside chunks of time when we allowed our answering machines to do exactly what we bought them for — take messages. We usually turn off all the ringers when we do this, because a phone ringing is just too much of a temptation.

Everyone has their own time wasters: those things that seem so necessary, you simply can't imagine not doing them. Many of them, laundry for example, *are* necessary, just not for as long or as frequently as most people manage to convince themselves.

c. Get enough sleep and exercise, and remember to eat

No matter how busy we get or what the deadline is, we've learned from hard experience that we need to get sleep, exercise, and food. It may be only a salad in front of the computer or a 15-minute walk around the park at the end of the street, but these things are essential to health and therefore to your ability to write.

d. Break the project into smaller bites

We're the kind of people who like to see a lot of items checked off on our daily "to do" lists, so we break tasks down into almost minuscule parts. Here's a typical example of a day's tasks as we approach the end of a short article on a Caribbean cruise.

(a) Finish closing paragraph

(b) Spell check

(c) Polish

(d) Confirm stats for sidebar

(e) Finalize sidebar

(f) Print article

(g) Notify editor

(h) Courier to editor

If we'd just assigned the tasks of (a) Finish article and (b) Send to editor, we'd feel as though we'd accomplished less.

If the sheer size of what you're working toward seems overwhelming, you probably need to break it into smaller pieces.

e. Indulge in a mini vacation — a day, a weekend, an hour

It can be as lavish as a weekend away with your best friend (which, of course, should give you some ideas for a great new article when you get back) or as simple as a candlelight dinner or bubble bath. A mini-vacation is about pampering yourself. So indulge and forget about writing for however long you've allowed yourself.

Some writing instructors, such as Kenneth Atchity (author of *A Writer's Time*), even suggest faithfully making this time for play and pampering part of every project's work schedule. At the end of each segment, you know you'll be able to reward yourself for a job well done.

f. Write something different

Try either beginning or polishing a different article altogether. Maybe you're working on a piece about medieval European castles. Take a break by spending an hour or two brainstorming a new, fluffy piece about Disneyland with a two year old. When you use this approach, you'll come back to the castles refreshed *and* feeling a sense of accomplishment about the 500 words you wrote on Mickey and Minnie Mouse.

Even tackling a different part of your current project can be an interlude that often yields some amazing results. Write a sidebar, a chapter to fit 100 pages from where you are now, even an "If You Go" section — anything to get your fingers flying over the keyboard again.

g. The endless edit syndrome

Many would-be writers suffer from one insidious form of procrastination: the endless edit syndrome. These writers edit their work forever. It's never quite long enough or short enough or polished enough or....In short, it's never perfect enough to send to an editor.

On the other hand, if you've been polishing your 1,500 word article on the Orient Express for more than a decade, you likely don't want to contemplate the possibility your work isn't in the same league as Marco Polo's jottings.

If you see yourself in this mirror, set a deadline for the proposal or manuscript to be submitted, and stick to it. No matter how badly you *think* it reads, send your work out on the date you've set. If it makes you feel better, have a professional editor go over it first, but get your manuscript in the mail on time!

16
To have and to hold
— forever

a. To keep or not to keep

You've contacted every tourist board you can think of, every chamber of commerce, every public relations company, every travel supplier on the continent, and you have subscriptions to every travel publication known to man, woman, or child. You are receiving every news release, press release, and brochure available in the world of travel, and then some.

Suddenly that cheerful soul who delivers your mail won't meet your eye any more. Those friendly exchanges are a thing of the past. Your letter carrier no longer has a upright bearing but posture bent under the weight of a mail bag. Your fault.

Your letter carrier may gripe but he or she has it easy. It's *your* office that's overrun with paper. You've nowhere to sit. You can't find anything and the wonderful ocean view that enticed you to purchase your home is completely obstructed by piles of unopened mail. What to do with all this stuff? What to file and what to keep?

Unfortunately, there's no simple answer. We know of a weekly columnist who limits the amount of information kept to a pile no higher than five inches. We also know a writer who does a lot of freelance work for travel industry publications whose basement is set up like a library, complete with row after row of eight-foot-high shelves filled with all manner of brochures and books. This writer keeps everything that arrives at the office for possible use later. If someone makes a last minute request, he doesn't have to budge from his home office. Everything is right there at his fingertips.

Your own decisions are based on what you write about. If you're producing a weekly column, you'll frequently be searching for information in spite of everything that arrives in the mail or on the fax machine. If you're a freelance writer frequently called on to write up a particular destination at short notice, you may decide to keep a wide range of source material. If so, plan to add travel books to the list arriving at your door.

What you keep may also depend on your space and how much paper you can tolerate in your life.

Deciding what to keep will become easier with time. Really. At first we kept everything, but didn't want to use valuable filing cabinet space on items of doubtful value. So the pile ended up in a huge mound in the corner of the office, all because of our fear of throwing out something valuable. One day, after realizing we hadn't gone through the pile in a number of months, we ruthlessly threw the lot out. We didn't read any of it. Didn't sort it. We just shovelled it into recycling bags. We haven't missed anything.

That said, you are the best person to decide what you need to keep. At first you may feel more comfortable keeping more than you need, just in case.

Be warned though. It is often easier to be put on a mailing list than to get off. Barbara learned that when she moved and carefully sent changes of address to endless lists of suppliers, tourist boards, etc. Sure enough the stream of mail started arriving at the new address. Did it stop at the old address? No. Kept going there too. About once a year it seems companies update their media lists and call to verify your address and your continuing interest in receiving material. They remove the old addresses at that time.

It is often easier to be put on a mailing list than to get off it.

b. Organize what you do keep

One summer while attending university, Barbara went to work as a temp in an office. The person who was training her had a quirk about what could be written on a file folder and how they should be used. It had to be typed and it had to contain information which was going to be kept in the office for quite a period of time. As a result, this person had little piles of paper which didn't really have a home all over her desk because she hadn't made her way over to the typewriter to neatly type up a label yet. Periodically she put all these pieces of paper into a miscellaneous file and felt content that all was right with the world. Until she had to find something.

Don't copy this mode of organizing. Chances are you are the only person who will read your files. So feel free to scribble anything that will be identifying to you on the top of the file. And use those files freely. They are relatively cheap if you buy in bulk at one of the office supply superstores.

We don't even have a miscellaneous file. If it is worth keeping, it's worth a file. You may not want a whole file on ostrich racing in Arizona, but slip that article into your Arizona file and you'll be able to find it when you need it. If you doubt your ability to find such an item when needed, you may want to set up a card file to reference where the data is stored. For example, you would put ostrich racing on a card file to be filed under "O." Also on the card you would write "see Arizona file." Problem solved.

Of course, you may be like Rick and Barbara. They loved the idea of ostrich racing so much that they wrote about it and got it into print right way. Never did have to find a place to file it. Again, problem solved.

If you are working on a project for only two days and it will make your life easier to use 15 files during that time to keep yourself organized, what difference does it make? When you are finished the project, simply slap a label over the old writing and the file is ready to use again. What could be simpler?

What kind of two-day project could require 15 files? You might be talking with a number of different suppliers and want a separate file for each. You may want to have a file for information you have read and discarded. You may want a file just for your sidebar material. You get the picture.

c. Filing systems

After you've been working with your travel material for a while, you'll decide what is most convenient for you.

A system of colored file folders and a filing cabinet should cover the basics. Using a separate color for travel suppliers, publications, destinations, particular projects, queries, business accounts, and any other categories you use frequently makes filing things away quicker and, therefore, it tends to get done. It also makes locating a particular file on a busy desk a less agonizing task.

We also use business card holders on our desk. What else to do with all those business cards we pick up or are sent to us?

We talk about setting up a database on the computer, but find we like to write notes on the cards as we talk to people on the phone. The number of free hours in our day does not make us want to transcribe the notes onto a computer afterward, nor do we want to type notes into the computer as we talk to people. It's one thing to silently write furiously as someone is telling you things — perhaps things they shouldn't — it's another to let them know you are doing so by the clicking of your keys.

d. Computer files

As you are organizing your office, don't forget that very important tool, your computer, if you use one. Word processing programs allow you to organize your files by directories, which helps to break down your mass of data into workable parts. You might want to have a directory for invoices, one for letters to editors, one for letters to sponsors, or even one for articles you are working on. You might want to call a directory Hawaii, and put in it all the work you are doing to promote the sale of an article: a letter to an editor, a letter to sponsor, thank-you notes.

But no matter how you organize your computer, back up your files regularly. Once a day is not too often. Consider having to redo your words of wisdom and it will be a terrific incentive to remember to do a backup.

And don't keep all your backups neatly piled beside your computer. Yes, you are protecting yourself against a system crash, but in case of fire or a break in, you could still find yourself without a backup. We solve the problem by sending a disk to a friend for safe keeping on a regular basis. We even store them in our car — anything to move all our valuable work off the premises.

Some time ago there was an item on the news about a man who had his computer stolen. He had been working on a program for eight years and it had been lost in the robbery. We can only assume he didn't have a backup. Don't let it happen to you.

Store a disk that you can boot your computer from with your backups. Windows and several other programs have the means to make a "system disk." Be sure to write-protect the disk by physically pulling the tabs on the side of the disk to the open position.

A system disk allows you to get back into your computer under certain circumstances without calling a repair technician. It doesn't repair your computer, but you might be able to sneak some data out of a crashed system and keep working. It is great insurance that has avoided potential disaster twice in our careers.

Also use a current antivirus program. You can purchase one at any computer store. These programs will help keep your files safe. This is especially important if you are accessing the Internet or swapping disks with other writers.

17

Equipping your office

a. A place to work

A pencil, a pad of paper, and, if you are human, an eraser, are all you need to start writing about travel. Many writers got their start at the kitchen table and composed works of art on scraps of paper. For years, Rick had a small desk in the living room serving as his writing corner. With a good set of earplugs, it worked fairly well.

But making a living as a writer is more than just writing, as the rest of this book has pointed out. Your kitchen table work space, pen and paper will frustrate you and everyone in your family eventually. It won't frustrate an editor because few editors will agree to edit handwritten manuscripts. So before you are asked to move into a hotel, consider spending a little time and money on these remedies.

A separate office for your writing is not essential and not always possible. But no matter how cramped your home is, you must set aside some space to keep the business side of your writing organized. You might be able to take your writing out to the front porch, but not all the little things like staplers, paper clips, and mailing labels which go along with a concerted mailing campaign transport easily. Pulling everything out and putting it all away again becomes a fatal obstacle to accomplishing even simple tasks.

Especially if you have children or a spouse, you will want a place you can leave all your work accessible. Whenever you have a spare minute you can come in and address an envelope before you go back to laundry or dinner. If you can close a door, even better.

The importance of having a desirable place to work

You may have a hard time justifying taking over the living room or closing off the rec room for hours at a time. But this is serious work and you deserve to give it the best possible chance to succeed.

If you have an entire room you can call your own, you're really in heaven. Make your office as pleasant as you can. Aim for inspirational — whatever that may mean to you. You will be spending a lot of time there, so whether you like posters of exotic destinations or fantasy art or silk flowers on wicker fans, indulge yourself. It's your space, make it somewhere you like being.

If you can, rent a separate apartment as an office or join with a like-minded group of writers to split the rent for a cheery space. We've tried both of these strategies and, at the time, they were a scary expense to add to our tight budget. In the end though, our production rose dramatically and it paid off.

Setting up an office can be fun if you like to shop. It is amazing what you can justify buying if it is for business. And the best part is you can write it all off. The government is helping you pay for all these things! On second thought, make a budget and stick to it. You don't want to have too much fun yet, and you do still need to pay for everything before you can write it off.

b. Telephone and fax systems

1. Telephone

One of your most important pieces of equipment is your telephone. Unlike fiction writing where you'll rarely need a phone, as a travel writer you'll be using one frequently to track down and verify information. Using your own home telephone line is fine, just answer in a straightforward, professional manner.

We prefer a separate line which we use only for business, and if you have a house full of teenagers, you will, too. Call waiting helps if you have a single line for personal and business calls, and it is cheaper than a second line. Just be sure your children know your calls take priority.

A phone extension in your office space is also a must. It makes for confusion if you have to make your calls in another room. As a quick solution, use a very long cord if you have only one phone or invest in a cordless phone. You can pick up extension cords at any electronics store.

You can use a simple phone with no bells and whistles, but we recommend a touch-tone phone with hold, redial, on-hook dialling, and a speaker phone. The speaker phone is essential. The first time you spend 20 minutes on hold with an airline using your head and

Many writers who set up their operation in basements find it is not conducive to work. They hate that buried feeling and the musty smell. Some find there's too little noise. They also tend to be cold in winter.

Basic office equipment list:

- *desk or writing surface of some kind*
- *adjustable chair*
- *computer and printer*
- *good light source*
- *filing cabinet*
- *telephone and phone books*
- *daily appointment calendar*
- *stationery: pens, paper, envelopes, postage stamps, paper clips, stapler, file folders, one or two three-ring binders, sticky notes, fax paper, blank stick-on address labels.*
- *maps or atlases*
- *good dictionary and thesaurus*
- *fax machine*

shoulder to grip the phone, you'll wish you'd gone with the hands-free feature. In Canada and the United States, you should pay no more than $160 for a speaker phone, and you can often find one on sale or at some of the discount stores for under $100.

2. Fax machine

You have two choices for your fax line. A dedicated line used exclusively for your fax machine or a combo line that handles both phone and fax. Dedicated lines are a must once you start receiving a heavy volume of news releases and queries. A dedicated fax line can also be used for outgoing calls in a pinch. So if you are waiting for a very important return call, you can still carry on with your research without tying up your regular phone.

However, when you are starting out, you can make do without one. Just be sure your fax machine is near your regular phone so when you pick up the receiver and hear that warbling sound you can start your fax without needing to run to the other room. Another option is to install a switcher to automatically differentiate between a fax tone and a regular phone call. These are readily available and cost just under $200.

Don't go overboard on a fancy fax machine. The extras we find consistently useful are a paper cutter, memory for when the paper runs out, and a document feeder. We also like the on-hook dialling feature.

A fax machine isn't hurt if it is left on all the time, and the amount of electricity used is minuscule. With it constantly on, it is ready to fax when you need, as well as receive incoming faxes as they come.

You may want to get a fax installed in your computer. Computer faxes require little training, and the initial cost of $100 or less will give you a modem as well (see section **e.**, below, for more on modems).

The drawback of computer faxes is that they are less flexible than a manual stand alone. While you can receive faxes from any source, you can fax out only those documents that are created as a file in your computer. It's great for saving paper because you can preview and print only the faxes you want to have a hard copy of, but you won't be able to fax a signed letter (unless you have scanned your signature into your computer) or fax copies of magazine and newspaper articles to people. You also can't fax back a signed copy of your contract to write an article.

So, even with a fax/modem for your computer installed, you may still need a conventional fax machine as well.

c. Answering machine or service

Who answers the telephone while you are out? If you have spent the whole morning on the phone trying to obtain information and have left countless messages on different voice mails, you can be sure everyone will call back the moment you walk out the door.

The easiest, most common solution is to buy an answering machine. You will miss a few calls because there are still people who are reluctant to leave messages, but overall, a recorded message is preferable to an endlessly ringing telephone. People want to call you once and pass on the information you requested, not phone you back a dozen times trying to reach you.

If you are using your home phone, remember to put a short professional-sounding message on your machine. Nothing puts business callers off more than having to listen to endless music and a long cutesy message before they can leave their name and number.

Voice mail and call-answer programs offered by most major telephone companies provide extra flexibility and have been steadily dropping in price over the past few years. In the long run they may still be more expensive than a basic answering machine, but they are often better suited to business requirements.

If you are sharing your phone with others, a voice mail that allows the caller to select to whom the message is going may be a good idea. You won't have to worry about not receiving your messages in their entirety.

Phone company services such as call alert, voice mail, and smart ring don't work if want to use one line for phone and fax. If you go this route, you will have to have a dedicated line.

d. Photocopier

To save money initially, use your fax machine as a copier. Most fax machines come with a copy feature which is sufficient for simple copies.

Personal copiers are the next step up and run $350 and higher. They tend to be slow and may have a limited range of paper sizes they can handle, but they are great for most of your needs.

Secondhand, reconditioned, or obsolete models can also be had at substantial savings. We don't recommend buying a service contract on a secondhand photocopier because they are expensive and, for small volume users, they are not good value. There are a lot of photocopier technicians out there who can help you if you have a breakdown.

A relatively new arrival in the marketplace are machines that combine fax, answering machine, photocopier, and laser printer. Basic models start at less than $1,000. Not only can this be a cost saving over buying four separate pieces of equipment, but the space saving factor is a major bonus.

e. *Computers*

Like any craftsman or artist, you need to have the proper tools. A computer with laser printer and the appropriate software is standard now for any business. Computers can save hours of your time drafting and re-editing an article to fit a particular publication's requirements. Although a computer will be the most expensive writing tool you have, the time it will save you in the editing stages will make your investment well worthwhile. Although there may be writers who still love the handwritten word on a yellow sheet of foolscap, there are not many magazine or newspaper editors who do.

If you consider yourself to be computer illiterate, check out the night school courses in your area for basic training. Learn a basic word processing program, such as Word or WordPerfect, and don't worry about anything else. The idea is to make your editing easier. Although it might be helpful, you don't have to learn all aspects of the computer.

When purchasing a computer, do stay with industry standards. Any store clerk can tell you if a piece of computer equipment is based on a standard. Namebrand computer equipment still commands a bit of a premium you really don't need to pay. Clones are so good now that you should feel quite safe purchasing something other than IBM computers.

There are thousands of people who regularly discard their six-month-old computer equipment the minute something bigger, better, and faster comes on the market. This means there are some incredible deals on secondhand computers for those who are willing to spend an hour or two looking. Used computers are cheap, often come with software already installed, and have had the bugs worked out by the previous owner. You may even be able to find an IBM XT computer or XT clone (an early model of home computer) which will give you all the basic editing capabilities for as little as $50. You may, however, have difficulty locating software for an XT, so make sure you know what you're getting before you buy. Look in your local newspaper, signboards in libraries, universities, or coffee shops for advertisements.

Newer computers with more memory and bigger hard drives use software that gives you many more options for laying out a snappy-looking proposal with pictures (graphics) and different styles of type (fonts). Unless you are going to be doing a lot of complex proposals, a newer model computer may be overkill.

New equipment with a warranty does give most people peace of mind. We recommend avoiding service contracts, because they tend to duplicate the warranty coverage when the machine is new. Some service contracts are so expensive they amount to prepaying for repairs on any breakdowns you might have. Computer repair and service has become highly competitive, and unless you live in an unusually isolated area, you should be able to locate a good repair service in the Yellow Pages.

1. Dedicated word processors

Halfway between an old-fashioned typewriter and a computer are dedicated word processors. They tend to look like large electronic typewriters and some even have small screens. Some are extremely inexpensive and allow you to do many of the same things a computerized word processor does.

We are biased toward computers since with one machine we can do accounting, word processing, keep our telephone book and a host of other things we like to use. However, dedicated word processors are slightly easier to learn, since you only have to learn about word processing commands, and not, for example DOS commands.

2. Software

We have used all kinds of word processors and each of us have a favorite. However, we can recommend all of the major word processing programs, since they all do the essentials. Even the very cheapest are a joy compared to writing with a pen, for us anyway.

If you find yourself in need of invoices or form letters for requesting information, you can design your own (called templates) on most word processing programs. By creating your own templates, you can modify each form to suit your own needs and preferences.

A word of caution: some of the older cheap word processing programs may not have a spell check. Spell checking is essential, especially if you are a rotten typist.

People tend to adjust to the idiosyncrasies of the word processor they use the most. For many years, we were perfectly happy to use a program without a back space delete key. If we wanted to omit what we'd just typed, we backed up to the beginning of the word and use the delete key.

3. Smaller and smaller

Laptop and notebook computers have put one of our dreams within reach. We now can sit in a beach side café and write, rather than always being cooped in the office. Great for a change of scene, and wonderful for drawing inspiration from little vignettes of life passing by.

Before you rush out to buy either one, consider the purchase carefully. Both laptop and notebook computers are considerably more expensive than a regular computer. While many writers wouldn't leave home without one, others prefer not to have to worry about the security needed for it when they travel. If you are writing on adventure travel, for example, a computer may be more of a hindrance than a help.

f. Communicating

E-mail and sending documents by modem is fast becoming the communication mode of choice among writers and editors. E-mail is the computer equivalent of an answering machine. You can leave a message for someone on his or her e-mail, which he or she can then read at a convenient time. The difference is that on this answering machine, you can leave entire manuscripts or pictures in addition to your message.

E-mail has even more in common with voice mail because you do not actually connect with the person's computer until he or she asks for messages from the central computer. The recipient's computer does not need to be on for you to leave a message.

People love e-mail because it allows them to communicate with someone without going through the social chitchat of a telephone call. Like an answering machine, it does give you some control over when you respond to other's requests. Some people swear it gives them greater periods of uninterrupted time than they used to have.

You can also electronically transfer a manuscript by modem. This is a direct computer-to-computer transfer of data without using e-mail. In this case, the recipient's computer does have to be on for you to send data. Not only is it useful for transferring finished articles instantaneously (no more worrying if the courier got it there on time), it is terrific for any kind of collaboration between editors and authors, or among co-authors. You can work on the manuscript and then hand it back electronically without leaving your office. It's like transferring data by disk, but faster.

More and more publications now accept manuscripts by modem. Some are reluctant to do it any other way. So if you are not computer literate, don't know e-mail from an elephant, your options as a writer are going to become narrower and narrower. If you want to be a regular contributor to a publication, you should start working on your electronic communicating skills right now.

Both e-mail and electronic transfer require you to have a piece of computer equipment called a modem. An internal modem fits neatly inside your computer while an external modem sits outside the computer case on your desk. Both types work equally well, though an internal modem will cost less because it doesn't need a case to live in.

You do not need to have fancy equipment to bring you into the 21st century. The horsepower of a modem is measured in bits per second (bps), a measure of the data transfer rate. The higher the number the better, especially if you want use the Internet.

A modem that transmits at 14.4 bps costs under $60 new and under $30 secondhand. Though not the latest or highest speed, it will work for Internet research and sending your files to a publisher.

As modems and other communications equipment become faster, try to stay at least a generation behind the newest advances. Computing history shows the generation of equipment that is becoming obsolete is still widely used but less sought after, and therefore, cheaper.

You will need to set up an account for e-mail with a local service provider (see your Yellow Pages under Computers or visit any computer store) or one of the big international companies like CompuServe or America Online. Most of these companies will entice you with some free hours and low rates for every hour you use. Shop around. Normally $10 a month buys you five to ten hours of on-line time, which is more than enough for e-mail.

Programs for e-mail are relatively easy to use and getting more user friendly all the time. If it all seems too much, contact your local school board or college about continuing education courses. These are inexpensive and helpful.

18
Copyright and other legal gremlins

Copyright is a curious subject, but one that will require a lot of thought in the future.

Stanley J. Nicol, *Scrivener*, Summer 1995

a. Copyright and your words

Copyright is probably the ugliest ogre most new writers attempt to face down. It is the source of nightmares and chewed fingernails for well over 50% of the students in every writing class. What happens if someone steals my article? How do I know an editor won't read my story and then assign it to one of the staff writers? What if...?

This book is not meant as a substitute for legal counsel. If you will feel confident your writing is safe and protected only if you resort to costly legal means, then for the sake of your own peace of mind, seek professional advice immediately. And when you reach the enviable stage in your career where publishers and editors are fighting among themselves for the privilege of publishing your work, there is no question you should retain a lawyer.

Until then, while you do need to be aware of copyright law and must be diligent when your rights are infringed on, basic copyright is not as terrifying, expensive, or abused as many writers believe. You will save yourself endless frustration, sleepless nights, and money by learning to resist the feeling that everyone is "out to get you and your ideas for free."

1. Copyright is automatic

Once you have committed your own original work into permanent form by writing it down, copyright is automatic. It is not necessary to indicate copyright with the copyright symbol (©), but in both Canada and the United States it does offer some extra degree of legal clout should your copyright ever be challenged. You may want to show the copyright symbol, your name, and the year the work was first produced on all your manuscripts. (**Note:** Some editors we've spoken with (both Canadian and American) feel showing the copyright symbol on your manuscript labels you as an amateur.)

2. You cannot copyright an idea

The words you use to express an idea are protected by copyright. No one can use the same words to describe the same idea without violating your copyright. However, the idea itself cannot be copyrighted. If three people decide to write about sailing around the world in a 30-foot sailboat, no one person could sue the other two for copyright infringement unless the words used to express that idea were identical.

3. Registering copyright

For a fee, you can register your copyright. In Canada, the cost is $35 and should be submitted to:

Copyright Office
Canadian Intellectual Property Office (CIPO)
5th Floor — 50 Victoria Street
Place du Portage, Tower I
Hull, QC K1A OC9

An application form should accompany the payment, but a copy of the actual work needn't.

In the United States, the cost to register copyright is $20. To order application forms, contact:

Copyright Office
Publications Section, LM-455
Library of Congress
Washington, DC 20559

An application form *and* a copy of the work will then need to be filed with the Register of Copyrights.

While at first glance these fees may not seem expensive, they add up rapidly. If you're producing no more than an article every two or

Both the United States and Canada are members of the Berne Convention, which means that if your copyright is protected in the United States, it is automatically protected in Canada (and any other country that is a member of the convention), and vice versa.

three weeks, you'll end up spending over $500 annually if you register them in either country.

Some writers, instead of registering copyright, mail themselves a double-registered copy of everything they write. If you elect to use this method, be sure to seal your envelope with clear tape and to write your signature across the flap (see Sample #15). When you receive your manuscript, tuck the unopened envelope away in your filing cabinet or safety deposit box as proof you were the original author.

This method is less expensive than registering all your work, but there is some question as to whether it is legally acceptable as proof of original authorship.

Sample #15
Labelling your envelope

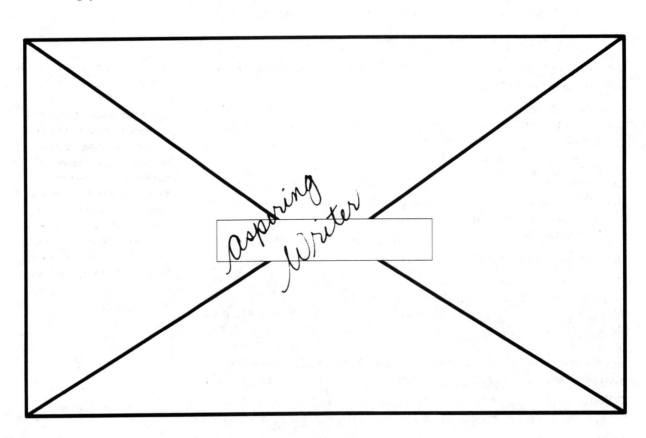

4. Work for hire

One aspect of copyright worth special attention is *work for hire.*

Let's say Travel Promotions and Publicity Inc. (TPP Inc.) wants you to review their newest, hottest hotel property on the British West Indies island of Anguilla. In this scenario you will be either:

(a) An employee of TPP Inc. You are paid an hourly or monthly wage by the company, you have all the usual payroll deductions taken from your salary at source, and you are eligible for any benefits it offers. The trip to Anguilla is one of the more pleasant among your many duties of employment.

or

(b) You are an independent freelancer hired by TPP Inc. on a per-job basis. You invoice TPP Inc., you must pay any legally required deductions yourself, such as government social security or unemployment plans, and you are not eligible for company benefits because you are not an employee of the company.

In the first scenario, your writing is considered to be part of your job, and the copyright remains with your employer unless you have a legal agreement otherwise.

In the second scenario, as a freelancer you will retain copyright to your material unless you have previously signed away those rights to TPP Inc.

Since most of you reading this book will fall into the category of independent contractor or freelance writer, this distinction will probably never affect you.

5. Keep up-to-date

It's crucial to remember that copyright law is constantly changing. Nowhere is this more noticeable than in the world of cyberspace. Copyright law has not caught up with the information superhighway. Lawyers and government regulatory boards are struggling to develop suitable and, more important, enforceable policies, but there is currently no easy way to enforce copyright of your work once it has been placed on the Net — a fact causing great concern to all artists. Often, you've effectively sold "all world rights" for zero dollars.

As an artist and as a businessperson, it is your responsibility to keep current and aware of copyright law and how it affects you.

One of the sad truths about writing is that many authors do not see themselves as business people. Somehow the idea they must learn about the legal and business aspects of what they do seems to diminish the luster of their career. However, writers who accept this as just one of the many skills they need are generally those whose careers shine brightest.

b. Selling the right rights

Unless your topic is time sensitive, wait six months after selling first serial rights, then relaunch your articles into the marketplace. Be sure to indicate in your cover letter where and when the story originally appeared and make it clear you are now offering reprint rights.

1. First serial rights

By far the most commonly sold rights (especially in the periodical marketplace), first serial rights give a certain publisher the right to publish your original work for the first time.

It's easy to see you cannot sell first rights more than once in overlapping geographical areas. If you've sold *North America Travel Magazine* the first North American serial rights for your article on cruising the Nile, you cannot sell the first California serial rights to *California Travel Magazine*. You could, however, sell first Australian serial rights to *Australia Travel Magazine*.

2. Second serial rights (reprint rights)

You can sell reprint rights to as many markets as are willing to accept your work once your story has appeared in print. Many small and/or regional publications regularly purchase reprint rights. While you will generally make less money than you did selling first serial rights, you don't have to write another article either.

You will learn from experience what you will get paid for what, and what amount is acceptable to you.

The amount you are paid has little to do with first or second or one-time rights. For example, if you sold the first rights or rights to only a local paper, you might get paid very little. The second rights, on the other hand, if sold to a major magazine, might get you considerably more.

Publishers who buy reprint rights for your article may publish that article more than once in some circumstances. Clarify in writing if this is the case.

3. One-time rights

One-time rights are generally used if you are selling the same article to several non-competing markets at the same time. For example, your Nile article could be published in *California Travel Magazine*, *New York Travel Magazine,* and *Yukon Travel Magazine* within weeks of each other.

The publisher that has bought one time rights from you can use the piece only once.

4. All rights

Selling all rights is a very big step with some very long-term consequences. Once you have signed away all rights, you have forfeited the right to use your article or book again in any format, including video, movie, anthology, or syndication. You've even given up the ability to use your own words in all future means of production *as yet undiscovered.*

As speculation increases about Internet publishing, some publishers are trying to hedge their bets about what is to come by asking for all rights. We've even run across one unscrupulous publisher who "bought" all rights, but offered no payment to his contributors (this, thankfully, is a rarity).

Our recommendation about all rights is simple: never sell all rights unless you are being paid so much money for them you will be able to retire in luxury as soon as you cash the check.

However, that said, everybody has to make decisions without being able to foresee the future. Perhaps in two years, with the benefit of hindsight, giving away the movie rights (included in all rights) to your travel guide won't seem so smart. You can try to negotiate your way around it when you sell the book, but if the deal hinges on the movie rights, you may decide to give up those possible sources of future revenue in favor of being published now. Your first book is one of the most important steps in your career and will open many other doors.

5. Book rights

Book rights are complex and each sale will be different. While there are many good books on the market about negotiating these sales, this is one area where you will probably want to seek legal advice.

c. The check's in the mail

1. When selling rights, be sure you know when you will be paid

Most magazines pay "on publication," that is, a week or two after the article appears in print. From the magazine's perspective, paying on publication means they don't have to prepay for editorial that may not appear in print for months. From the writer's perspective, it means a wait of sometimes a year or more after submitting an article before there's a financial return for the hours spent writing.

Many writers, quite justifiably, feel this is an unfair practice. After all, they can't market first serial rights of their work elsewhere during this waiting period. Unfortunately, it's often the only way to get paid anything for your travel articles.

If you can, negotiate to be paid on acceptance and you'll see a check as soon as the publication has accepted your final copy. Susan was lucky to sell her first professional article to a magazine that paid on acceptance. She received her check in February, even though the piece didn't appear in print until November. However, there are very few editors who pay first timers on acceptance; some pay even regular contributors only on publication.

Occasionally, a magazine will ask for an invoice to process your payment. While this is uncommon, be sure to check with the editor or accounting department ahead of time. Sample #16 shows how you can set up your own invoice.

Regardless of how you are to be paid, your best bet is to stay on top of what is happening to your manuscript. If the check does not appear when it was scheduled to, phone and find out why. Has your article been rescheduled for a later issue or has it been scrapped altogether?

2. The kill fee

No, this is not the amount paid to your survivors if you are flattened by a Bangkok trucker. A kill fee is the amount (usually based on a percentage of the original payment negotiated) that the magazine will pay you if it decides not to run the article after committing to publishing it. Not all publications pay kill fees.

Sometimes you do not even need to write the article to earn the kill fee. Once, shortly after Barbara and Rick were assigned an article, the editor left and the new editor decided to do something very different with the magazine. They received a check without writing a word.

Generally, if an article isn't going to be published, all rights revert to you even if the article was submitted before the publisher decided to kill it. However, be sure to confirm what your contract stipulates; sometimes the kill fee also kills your ability to market the piece elsewhere.

3. When you don't get paid at all

It happens. Your article on Caribbean sunsets is published and months go by without payment. Finally, a crestfallen editor calls to tell you the magazine is out of business and you are now an unsecured creditor of a company with no assets. Or the magazine was purchased by another company and the new and former owners are arguing over who is supposed to pay the writers for previous articles. (Both true stories.)

You can get angry, but you probably do not want to get even. You *do* have every right to sue and you can sometimes harass owners into paying without going to court. But as writers who have a difficult

Dick Tyler
123 Main Street
Anytown, BC X5V 3Y7

January 15, 199-

Lois Jordan
Managing Editor
Let's Travel
789 Lesser Street
Your Town,   AB   X5X 4X2

INVOICE

For travel article "Sailing the 'Sundays" published in the spring edition of *Let's Travel*.

Total due: $1,500.00

Thank you.

Sincerely,

Dick Tyler

Dick Tyler

time smiling when someone steps on us, we can tell you that in this business, it is sometimes smart to just "grin and bear it."

First, even if you win a judgment, magazines and papers usually don't have much in the way of assets you can attack. Second, you'll expend more emotional energy trying to recover your paycheck than it is worth. You could spend the same energy much more positively advancing your career by finding another buyer. Lastly, editors do not go down with the company. They move to other magazines where they will hire you because they know not only that you do publishable work but you also are a kind and understanding sort who gave them a break in one of their more embarrassing moments.

d. Protecting yourself

Because magazines contract for articles months ahead, there is usually time to do a bit of negotiation about the terms of the sale. Don't be afraid to ask for changes.

Many magazines don't use written contracts and rely on a verbal agreement between writer and editor. While reputable publications will follow through, be aware that verbal contracts protect you less (in some cases not at all) because if there is a disagreement, it becomes one person's word against the other's. There is also the problem about how one person interprets what was said.

To protect yourself from confusion, write a short letter outlining the terms as you understand them and mail it to the publisher. Make sure you detail the deadline, payment, subject, and length of the article and the rights you are selling them. At the end write the sentence, "If this is not what we have agreed, please let me know right away." Keep a copy for your files. See Sample #17 for an example.

Book contracts are discussed in detail in chapter 10.

H. Melville Publishing
1234 Whalers Meuse
Boston, MA 55566

Dear Mr. Dick:

I am so pleased you like the hook in the first line of the story! I am really excited about the prospects of writing a 500-word article entitled "Where to Find the Tastiest Shark Sandwiches Around the World" for your "Unusual Eats" column for the August 199- issue of *Small Boat Traveler*. The article will give readers specific restaurant recommendations and the sidebar will contain at least one toothsome recipe.

I understand that the deadline for submission is April 1, 199-. The payment is $500 and I am to bear all research and medical costs. You are purchasing first serial rights for North America only and there is no kill fee.

If this is not what we have agreed, please let me know right away.

It was great to see you on that cruise out of Boston last year. We'll have to go fishing again sometime.

Cheers,

Captain Ahab

Captain Ahab (RET)

19
Play money and taxing questions

We have a hobby that is closely tied to travel writing that we want to share with you. It requires imagination, is intellectually stimulating, will compel you to read arcane books to ferret out the secrets of a mysterious, largely hidden organization, and will then pit you against some of that organization's most hideous minions. It's a real-world game with big prizes and stiff penalties. Some aficionados make enough each year to pay for their kid's college, while a greedy few risk too much and are forced to sell their homes. Oh, and there's one other important thing about this hobby. Spouses generally become enthusiastic players themselves once they have studied the rules and enjoyed the payback from winning a few rounds.

No, it is not lingerie dungeons and dragons. We collect receipts.

You know, those things waiters give you after dinner, the last unused coupon of your airline ticket, the best reason to carry a credit card.

Especially at the beginning of your career, you'll probably get more money back from write-offs than you'll make from your writing, possibly thousands of dollars each year. And it's all perfectly legal.

Collecting receipts is like collecting money.

a. The rules of the game

(a) Collecting receipts is an exciting and stimulating game of intrigue and mental agility that pits you against the nefarious henchmen of the tax department. The tax collector starts the game by insisting you turn over up to 52% of everything you earn. (This is the Canadian version of the game, which is much rougher than the U.S. version.)

(b) As the tax collector advances on your assets, you use receipts to keep them out of his sticky grasp. Some receipts work better than others. Some can land you in jail, the Supreme Court, or before bankers asking for emergency financing.

(c) You can add to your cash stash if you can decipher the mysteries of the "tome of the tax code." This book discloses in the form of riddles and enigmas the mysterious path to saving your assets. Fail, and up to half of everything disappears just after April Fools' Day each year.

(d) The player who keeps the most without lying, wins.

(e) Ages 18 to 105. Calculator batteries not included.

b. Tips on game strategy

The key to winning is to collect only those receipts that keep the tax collector at bay. Distinguishing these from the ones which have no effect or a detrimental effect is the magical art.

Learn the general principles that will tell you which ones to ignore. Presenting some receipts to the tax collector, such as the one for the flowers for your daughter's wedding, is considered cheating and encourages them to review past years' games. This is to be avoided.

Keep good records and your receipts in one place. An old shoe box will do nicely.

Do not bluff or deceive. Use superior logic. The surest way to lose in future years is to not tell the tax collector everything. Besides, the game is fairly easy to win if you read the "tax tome" (or the cheater notes that come with your tax forms).

Hire a sorcerer accountant. Disguised as normal human beings, these savants of the tome can give you the right spells and subsections for all situations. No one should battle the tax collector without one. Your payment offerings of chickens, cash, or checks to your accountant will be well spent and are tax deductible in next year's game.

Keep good records and your receipts in one place. An old shoe box will do nicely. Fanatical players love to arrange and rearrange their receipts in categories but we find this isn't necessary. It's kind of like putting all your baseball cards in an album. Albums are great for show, but what really counts is actually having the cards. As long as you collect receipts you are in the game. However, the very best players organize them.

Read up on various tax incantations such as the guidelines for artists and writers or writing off your home.

Gain an appreciation for depreciation.

c. Identifying receipts as jail bait or gems

Travel writers should keep receipts pertaining to vacations, home expenses, eating out, and auto expenses.

1. Vacations

The term "vacation" is a misnomer since travel writers never take vacations. Every trip is a research trip. Just because you enjoyed flying the jets of the Russian Air Force so much you would have paid to do it does not mean you weren't punching a clock. You were working hard.

Travel to exotic places is the biggest item you can write off that most other people can't. Guard these very collectible receipts carefully.

(a) Before the trip.

Collect receipts for research books on the destination, vaccinations, trip interruption insurance, cancellation insurance, supplemental overseas medical insurance, camera and baggage insurance, accident insurance, rental car insurance, and snake bite insurance (just kidding).

(b) During the trip

Collect receipts for expenses for transportation to or car parking at the airport/cruise terminal, baggage handling tips, magazines to read on the plane (for research), a snack while waiting to depart, any departure taxes, a cab to your hotel, your hotel and meals, your scuba lessons, horseback riding, snorkel gear rental, sun screen, sunglasses and string bikini (protective work wear), drinks and dinner for anyone you interview, the grand tour around the island, any magazines, papers, or research postcards (instead of trying to always find out the spelling of each temple, buy postcards). Whew. Are you getting the idea?

(c) Write off your spouse

If your spouse takes a photograph or two that appear with your article, keep all his or her receipts, too. Better yet, put your spouses's name on the article.

(d) Support child labor

If you write articles for parenting or family magazines on traveling with children, or popular children's destinations such as Disneyland, Universal Studios, Club Med, dude ranches, certain cruises (The Big Red Boat, for instance), you naturally have to take children along in order to write convincingly about the experience, so keep their receipts. After all, isn't it about time they worked for a living?

(e) After the trip

Thank-you cards and "When can I come see you again?" follow-up phone calls produce legitimate receipts for the tax collector.

2. Home expenses

The second biggest write off available to travel writers is the expenses related to a home office. You can write off part of your rent or mortgage payments if you follow the rules. The U.S. government is particularly finicky about how you do this and the Canadian government is tightening up too. You should be able to make a deduction as long as you:

(a) set aside a whole separate room (in the U.S. an area of your den or part-time on the kitchen table won't satisfy) or portion of a room (in Canada);

(b) use it exclusively for your work (no sewing machines, televisions, spare beds or personal storage allowed); and

(c) use it as your principal place of business (you can't have an office downtown for your writing business, although you can still go to a place of work downtown for someone else or for a different business).

It does help immensely to establish the room's use as a business deduction if you meet clients and business associates or conduct interviews in the room and have a separate phone line.

When deducting your home office expenses, you may be able to write off portions of your heating and air conditioning, cleaning, painting, property tax, rent or mortgage interest (if you can't already), and house insurance.

- *stationery*
- *advertising*
- *printing, copying*
- *postage, courier, telephone*
- *auto, parking*
- *home rent, repairs, mortgage*
- *insurance*
- *travel*
- *research material*
- *computer equipment and software*
- *office furniture*
- *accounting and legal fees*
- *dues for professional associations*
- *conference fees*
- *Internet charges*
- *restaurants or even meals in your home if you entertain for business associates*
- *banking charges*
- *camera equipment*
- *photographs and film*
- *gifts*
- *payment to research assistants*
- *equipment repair*
- *lease payments for equipment*
- *cable TV (CNN and travel shows are a great source of information)*
- *library fees*
- *interest on a business loan*
- *portion of home repairs or maintenance such as grass cutting*

You do need to talk to your accountant to be sure exactly what you can and cannot do. In Canada, for instance, the tax collector may be able to grab part of the proceeds of the sale of your home if you do major renovations and try to write them off. Depreciating the renovations may interfere with your principal residence tax exemption on the capital gain on your home.

3. Eating out and auto expenses

Eating out is one area where the tax collector would like to take a bite out of you. So many people take friends out to dinner and try to write it off — the tax collector watches these expenses closely. If you discuss business at lunch, keep detailed notes about who attended and what you discussed.

Automobile deductions require even more record keeping. Usually this includes keeping a mileage log of both personal and business use. If you rarely need your car to do business, you might consider forgoing the deduction and record keeping. Your gas, oil, maintenance, and insurance are normal deductions.

Be sure to talk to your accountant about the rules for writing things off. The rule of thumb is that it must be directly related to earning money. Most items you can deduct in full but a few, such as automobiles, restaurants, rent, and equipment expenses, have special rules you must comply with.

d. A business or a hobby?

Collecting receipts can be a great hobby once you know how much money they can bring you. However, you can deduct these expenses only if your business has a reasonable chance of eventually generating income for you.

Nobody really knows if you can generate a living from your writing. Maybe you are ahead of your time and your hard hitting, investigative style of writing children's travel stories just is not popular yet. Who knows what the fashion may be in a few years?

So, to convince the tax collector your efforts to earn money are sincere, it helps to:

- Sell some articles each year.
- Show evidence you really are trying. Evidence can be query letters and proposals sent and articles written.

- Collect research on trips. Brochures, rate sheets from hotels, pictures suitable for an article all help to prove the case that you are a hard-working journalist.
- Join professional associations and your local chamber of commerce.
- Open a bank account for your earnings and expenses.

e. Finding an accountant

While some writers prefer to have an accountant look after their financial planning and bookkeeping, many would rather do their own. It gives them a chance to see how their writing business is going. For help, keep handy the phone number of the local tax office to order government information booklets and talk with government tax advisers who will answer most of the questions you may have. This strategy can save you a bundle of money in accounting fees.

Our accountant understands we want to do our own taxes but just need a little advice from time to time and is happy to work with us on that basis. We highly recommend hiring an accountant. At some point you will need someone you can turn to.

20
In closing

Life is either a daring adventure or nothing at all.
Helen Keller

Now you have reached the end of this book, your true journey begins. We hope you have found inspiration and new ideas within these pages. We wish you success in your writing and joy in your travels as you take the first step down the road to your own daring adventure.

Bon chance and bon voyage!

Appendix
Resources

These lists are in no way complete, but they will give you some idea of what's out there.

a. Publications

1. Useful travel publications

Best Fares Discount Travel Magazine
Box 14261
Arlington, TX 76094-1261
Toll free: 1-800-635-3033
Fax: (817) 860-1193

Canadian Travel Press
310 Dupont Street
Toronto, ON M5R 1V9
Tel: (416) 968-7252

Condé Nast Traveler
360 Madison Avenue
New York, NY 10017
Tel: (212) 880-8800
Fax: (212) 880-2190

Consumer Reports Travel Letter
Box 53629
Boulder, CO 80322-3629
Toll free: 1-800-234-1970

Islands
Islands Publishing Company
3886 State Street
Santa Barbara, CA 93105-3112
Tel: (805) 682-7177
Subscriptions: 1-800-284-7958

National Geographic Traveler
4th floor, 1145 17 Street NW
Washington, DC 20036
Tel: (202) 857-7000
Subscriptions: 1-800-775-6700

The Thrifty Traveler
Box 8168
Clearwater, FL 34618
Toll free: 1-800-532-5731

Tour & Travel News/TTG North America
Box 1190
Skokie, IL 60076
Toll free: 1-800-447-0138

Travel Impulse
Sun Tracker Enterprises Ltd.
319 - 7231 120 Street
Delta, BC V4C 6P5
Tel: (604) 951-3238
Fax: (604) 951-8732

Travel Holiday
1633 Broadway
New York, NY 10019
Tel: (212) 767-5101

Travel & Leisure
1120 Avenue of the Americas
New York, NY 10036
Tel: (212) 382-5600
Fax: (212) 768-1568

Travelweek Bulletin
Travel Trade Publication
282 Richmond Street E., Suite 100
Toronto, ON M5A 1P4
Toll free: 1-800-727-1429

or

163 — 07 Depot Road
Box 188
Flushing, NY 11358
Tel: (718) 939-2400
Fax: (718) 939-2047

2. Useful resource publications

Books in Print
An updated version of this reference book is
available at most libraries.

Canadian Markets for Writers and Photographers
Proof Positive Productions Ltd.
#1330 – 194 – 3803 Calgary Trail
Edmonton, AB T6J 5M8
Fairly new, but extensive and easy to read.

Canadian Writer's Market
McClelland & Stewart
481 University Ave
Toronto, ON M5G 2E9
Lists magazines, book publishers, literary
agents.

*Gale Directory of Publications and
Broadcast Media*
Gale Research Company
835 Penobscot Building
Detroit, MI 48226-4094
Toll free: 1-800-877-4253
Tel: (313) 961-2242
Fax: (313) 961-6083
Extensive but expensive. An updated version
of this reference book is available at most li-
braries.

Producing a First-Class Newsletter
Self-Counsel Press
1481 Charlotte Road
North Vancouver, BC V7J 1H1

or

1704 N. State Street
Bellingham, WA 98225

Quill and Quire
70 The Esplanade, 2nd Floor
Toronto, ON M5E 1R2
Tel: (416) 360-0044
Fax: (416) 360-8745
Monthly journal for the Canadian book trade.

The following six publications are available from R.R. Bowker Company (see address below) or from the reference section of the library:

- *Books in Print Database*
- *International Literary Market Place*
- *Literary Market Place*
- *Publishers, Distributors and Wholesalers of the U.S.*
- *Publishers Trade List Annual*
- *Ulrich's International Periodicals Directory*

R.R. Bowker Company
121 Chanlon Road
New Providence, NJ 07974
Toll free: 1-800-521-8110
Tel: (908) 464-6800

Standard Periodical Directory
Oxbridge Communications
150 Fifth Avenue, Suite 302
New York, NY 10011-4311
Tel: (212) 741-0231
Fax: (212) 633-2938

The following three books are updated annually and are available from *Writer's Digest Books* (see address below):

- *Writer's Market: where and how to sell what you write*
- *Photographer's Market*
- *Guide to Literary Agents*

Writer's Digest Books
F&W Publications
1507 Dana Avenue
Cincinnati, OH 45207
Toll free: 1-800-543-4644
Tel: (513) 531-2222
Fax: (513) 531-4744

Writer's Digest Magazine
PO Box 2124
Harlan, IA 51593-2313
Fax: 1-800-333-0133
Subscription department (monthly)

b. Organizations

American Society of Journalists and Authors
1501 Broadway, Suite 220
New York, NY 10036
Tel: (212) 997-0947

Canadian Association of Journalists
St. Patrick's Building, Room 316B
Carlton University
1125 Colonel By Drive
Ottawa, ON K1S 5B6
Tel: (613) 526-8061
Fax: (613) 521-3904

Canadian Authors Association
27 Doxsee Ave N.
Campbellford, ON K0L 1L0
Tel: (705) 653-0323
Fax: (704) 653-0593

International Food, Wine and Travel Writers Association
Box 13111
Long Beach, CA 90803
Tel: (310) 433-5969
Fax: (310) 438-6384

International Women's Writing Guild
Box 810, Gracie Station
New York, NY 10028-0082
Tel: (212) 737-7536

National Writer's Association
1450 South Havana, Suite 424
Aurora, CO 80012
Tel: (303) 751-7844

National Writers Union
113 University Place, 6th Floor
New York, NY 10003
Tel: (212) 254-0279

Periodical Writers Association of Canada
54 Wolseley Street, Suite 203
Toronto, ON M5T 1A5
Tel: (416) 504-1645
Fax: (416) 703-0059

Society of American Travel Writers
4101 Lake Boone Trail, Suite 201
Raleigh, NC 27607
Tel: (919) 787-5181

Writers Guild of Canada
Third Floor North
35 McCaul Street
Toronto, ON M5T 1V7
Toll free: 1-800-567-9974
Tel: (416) 979-7907
Fax: (416) 979-9273

The Writers' Union of Canada
National Office
24 Ryerson Avenue
Toronto, ON M5T 2P3
Tel: (416) 703-8982
Fax: (416) 703-0826

Pacific Regional Office
3102 Main Street
Vancouver, BC V5T 3G7
Tel: (604) 874-1611

OTHER BUSINESS TITLES FROM SELF-COUNSEL

START AND RUN A PROFITABLE TOUR GUIDING BUSINESS

Part-time, full-time, at home, or abroad: your step-by-step business plan

Barbara Braidwood, Susan M. Boyce, and Richard Cropp

$14.95

For most people, traveling for free to exotic locales is just a fantasy. Whether you want to travel year-round or for two weeks every summer, from tropical climates to icy mountaintops, from luxury hotels to backpacks and hiking boots, tour guiding is one route to traveling where you want to go when you want to. This career demands creativity, planning, and sometimes endless patience, but you set your own timetable and pursue your own itinerary.

The authors provide background information on the travel industry, describe what is involved in tour guiding, explain how to develop tours to your favorite destination, and outline the planning you must do no matter where you are going. They also include a blueprint for the entrepreneur who wants to establish a larger tour operation.

The book answers questions such as:

- What should I think about when I plan a bus tour? A cruise?
- Where do I find the answers to tour members' questions?
- How do I deal with lost luggage or disorderly tourists?
- How can I market and advertise my tour?
- Should I sell my tour through a travel agency?
- What are the industry's standard commissions?

START AND RUN A PROFITABLE FREELANCE WRITING BUSINESS

Your step-by-step business plan

Christine Adamec

$14.95

Imagine being paid to do something you love — writing. As a freelance writer, you can work at home and be your own boss. But before you set up as an entrepreneurial writer, you need to consider the business side of writing.

Writing is a business and to be successful at it, you have to be an effective self-promoter, an able negotiator, a tireless researcher, and a talented writer. This book will help you decide whether a career as a freelance writer is for you, and it guides you through each step to success. It includes:

- Skills and traits of the successful writer
- Advantages of becoming a freelancer
- Knowing when to quit your day job
- Setting up an earnings plan and setting financial goals
- Choosing and researching your topic
- Effective interviewing techniques
- Successful networking
- Developing a loyal client base
- Learning when to say "no" to a project
- Setting rates and getting paid

PRACTICAL TIME MANAGEMENT

How to get more things done in less time

Bradley C. McRae

$7.95

Here is sound advice for anyone who needs to develop practical time management skills. It is designed to help any busy person, from any walk of life, use his or her time more effectively. Not only does it explain how to easily get more things done, it shows you how your self-esteem will improve in doing so. More important, emphasis is placed on maintenance so that you remain in control. Whether you want to find extra time to spend with your family or read the latest bestseller, this book will give you the guidance you need — without taking up a lot of your time!

Some of the skills you will learn are:

- Learning to monitor where your time goes
- Setting realistic and attainable goals
- Overcoming inertia
- Rewarding yourself
- Planning time with others
- Managing leisure time
- Finding time for physical fitness
- Planning time for hobbies and vacations
- Maintaining the new you

PRODUCING A FIRST-CLASS NEWSLETTER

A guide to planning, writing, editing, design, photography, production, and printing

Barbara A. Fanson

$14.95

Today, anyone with a computer can produce a well-designed newsletter. Fanson, an award-winning newsletter publisher, deals with every step of the process, from page layout to production schedules, editing to typesetting. Also included are valuable suggestions for writing, choosing photos and graphics, and working with a printer.

This is the definitive book on newsletter publishing, one that shows how to create a professional quality product.

Contents include:

- Getting your newsletter started
- Choosing what kind of newsletter you need
- Planning with a purpose
- Format: setting a style
- Building a functional format
- What you need to know about type
- Color
- Content: informing and entertaining the reader
- Good writing for great newsletters
- Writing headlines
- Legal considerations
- Desktop publishing and basic elements of design

PREPARING A SUCCESSFUL BUSINESS PLAN

A practical guide for small business

Rodger Touchie, B.Comm., M.B.A.

$14.95

At some time, every business needs a formal business plan. Whether considering a new business venture or rethinking an existing one, an effective plan is essential to success. From start to finish, this working guide outlines how to prepare a plan that will win potential investors and help achieve business goals.

Using worksheets and a sample plan, readers learn how to create an effective plan, establish planning and maintenance methods, and update their strategy in response to actual business conditions.

Contents include:

- The basic elements of business planning
- The company and its product
- The marketing plan
- The financial plan
- The team
- Concluding remarks and appendixes
- The executive summary
- Presenting an impressive document
- Common misconceptions in business planning
- Your business plan as a tangible asset

MARKETING YOUR SERVICE BUSINESS

Plan a winning strategy

Jean Withers and Carol Vipperman

$12.95

To effectively sell the service you offer, you must let people know that you exist and that you are better than your competition. This book explains what is necessary to develop a marketing plan that will work for service businesses ranging from law firms and dental practices to hair salons and auto repair shops. Whether your service is consulting or running a restaurant, you will profit from expanding your market.

The authors, consultants to service businesses, have provided 32 worksheets for you to develop your own specific marketing plan based on the procedures they describe.

The book answers the following questions:

- How does marketing a service differ from marketing a product?
- How do you prepare for marketing?
- Where can you find information about potential clients?
- What should you know about your competition?
- How do you establish goals that are desirable and realistic?
- What strategies for pricing and promotion will work best for you?
- How do you develop and implement an action plan for marketing?

WRITING ROMANCE

Create a bestseller from spark to finish

Vanessa Grant

$15.95

Have you ever read a romance novel and thought, "I could do this?" Considering that half of all paperbacks sold in North America are romance novels, generating over $885 million per year, writing about love can be big business! From plotting and characterization to editing and selling your manuscript, this book shows you how you can realize your creative dream and make money, too. Includes many examples from published romance novels, as well as a helpful resource guide useful for both new and experienced writers.

Learn how to —

- Develop believable characters
- Overcome writer's block
- Write romantic scenes
- Set up a suspenseful story
- Research your plot details
- Use your computer to write most efficiently
- Work with an agent
- Find a publisher
- Sell your book

ORDER FORM